Through the writings and personal teachings of Vernon Kitabu Turner, members of our Zen community have experienced fresh opening to the wonder of life. Kitabu manifests compassion in an infectious fashion that allows us to open ever more to our true nature.

Rev. Mitchell Doshin Cantor,
The Southern Palm Zen Group

"All candidates for black belt at my school are now required to read Soul Sword."

Master Dennis Brown,
Director of the U.S. Capitol Classics Tournament,
and founder of the Dennis Brown Shaolin Wushu Academy

Vernon Kitabu Turner speaks from that source within; that same source that inspires all great artists, masters, and teachers. His words reflect the truth of what is possible when one acts from that source.

Patrick Cassidy Sensei,
Director, Aikido of Fresno

BOOKS BY VERNON TURNER

Kung Fu: The Master

The Secret of Freedom

SOUL SWORD

SECOND EDITION

*The Way and Mind
of a Zen Warrior*

VERNON KITABU TURNER

HAMPTON ROADS
PUBLISHING COMPANY, INC.

For information write:
Hampton Roads Publishing Company, Inc.
1125 Stoney Ridge Road
Charlottesville, VA 22902

Or call: 804-296-2772
FAX: 804-296-5096

e-mail: hrpc@hrpub.com
Web site: www.hrpub.com

If you are unable to order this book from your local
bookseller, you may order directly from the publisher.
Quantity discounts for organizations are available.
Call 1-800-766-8009, toll-free.

Library of Congress Catalog Card Number: 00-103825
ISBN 1-57174-151-8

11 10 9 8 7 6 5 4 3 2

Printed on acid-free paper in Canada

the

great master

is

within you.

CONTENTS

SUKI: PUSH-BUTTON FEAR

A dancing flame is fascinating; to a child it is attractive, inviting to the touch. Those who fall prey to fire's seductive charm learn in an instant that it has a memorable bite. One touch is usually enough for children to learn to keep their hands away from it. Uncontrolled, fire can consume our property and worse. On the other hand, guided by our intelligence, we can use fire to cook our food, warm our bodies, and aid us in many other ways. Fire is neither good nor evil. It must be understood. The child who is terrified of fire will not act wisely in an emergency. If a parent teaches a child well, he will learn about the properties of fire, what to do and what not to do, even how to extinguish it if something goes wrong. Fear is learned. The images he sees and the words he hears impress upon the young mind and form impressions which may last for a lifetime.

There will always be those who abuse power, even if that power is falsely perceived, derived from superior height or muscular strength. Children are often taught that the bigger child, the stronger child, is to be feared in a confrontation merely by virtue of his or her physical attributes. In this way, children learn falsely that bodily strength alone is power. A child who believes in the superior force of the bigger child will give up lunch money and obey the commands of a bully because he has been taught that he is powerless against him. The bully senses this weakness. He knows exactly which victim to pick on when he needs a rush of "power" or a tasty lunch.

When I was a young boy, I liked to spend time alone and read. Sometimes I would find a nice spot under a tree and enjoy a book in its shade. To some of the other boys, I was therefore a wimp, a target to be assaulted. When the lead bully would punch me, I did not strike back. I found myself sensing the coming blows, but I refused to respond. Instead, I looked about frantically for someone to come to my rescue. Rarely did help come. I took the blows one by one until the bully was satisfied with himself. Sometimes I was struck in the stomach, but most of the time the favorite target of bullies would be the mouth or the eyes. Blows to either were painful and impossible to conceal. Lips swell when struck, eyes puff up and close. I did not understand why a human being could be so cruel to another person. I should have asked myself a different question: Why did I let another human being do such things to me?

The truth is that I feared the big fists of the bully. He was larger and apparently stronger than I; thus it was obvious to everyone that he would win. Yet each time someone fought me, I could feel the moves I should make—but I was too afraid to try them. Suppose I failed? The bully would be furious and hurt me even more. I continued to take punishment for being a bookworm.

During those days before I began to study the Warrior Way in earnest, there was an incident that clearly demonstrated an important principle, although it would be years before I recognized what that principle was. A well-known neighborhood scoundrel and his friends came over to our house and attacked my brother right in front of me. I wanted to defend him, but he had already proven he could whip me at will. Suddenly, I looked over my shoulder and saw my father peeping at the scene from behind the door. At once, realizing I could not embarrass my family, I turned and leapt into the air, landing heavily upon the boy I had feared only moments before.

My surprise maneuver knocked him off of my brother. In seconds, I had punched the bully into submission. His friends carried him away in tears. Dad praised me for coming to the aid of my little brother. It was the first fight I had ever won—and the last, for a long while. What caused my victory? We will explore the reason a little later.

The Tailor-Samurai

In feudal Japan, a tailor desired to travel to another province. He thought it would be wise to dress as a samurai warrior for his protection. No sooner had he arrived at his destination than he accidentally bumped a real samurai. The man was indignant. "You have dishonored me. Meet me at the edge of town at noon and we will settle this with swords," he said. The tailor was taken aback by the turn of events; he was no warrior. A few moments later, he wandered into the presence of a Zen Master. He related the story to him and asked for some insight into how he could face his fate with dignity.

"Do you study some discipline?" the monk asked.

"I am a tailor," he said.

"How do you approach your work?" the monk questioned.

The tailor explained how he focused on each task with singleness of mind.

"When you face your samurai today, do not regard him as he stands before you. Instead, use your tailor's mind to focus completely as you take off your outer coat and fold it neatly. Then tie up the sleeves of your shirt to get them out of your way. When you rise, close your eyes and draw your sword straight above your head, concentrating all your energy upon this act. At the first sign of movement from your enemy, bring your sword straight down. If you feel a cool breeze on top of your head, that will be death." The tailor thanked the Master for his instruction.

When the tailor arrived at the scene of the duel, he ignored those who had come to watch him and his opponent. Following the instructions of the Zen Master, he approached the fight as if he were in his shop working on clothes. He took off his outer coat with singleness of mind and remained focused throughout each act. Finally, he drew his sword high above his head and closed his eyes. The samurai had been watching with awe. He had never seen a warrior so meticulous about his garment or so unconcerned when facing death. He surmised that he was facing a great Master. He bowed. "I have been too hasty. I realize now that you did not bump me on purpose. There is no need for us to fight."

When the tailor later told the Zen Master what had happened, he was curious about the samurai's reaction. The Master explained, "He saw no fear of death in you. He could not sense your weakness . . . and so his own fear came to the surface." The tailor now understood the essence of the Warrior Way. Do you?

When faced with danger, most people react with self-consciousness. "I am going to be hurt," they think. Their responses then become tainted by the fear of pain and suffering and the desire to avoid them. The mind is divided between two distinctly different functions, taking decisive action and worrying about the consequences of failure. If you dwell on the pain and suffering, you increases the likelihood of those very results. Fearing the worst is not in itself a preventative. If you wobble between fear and taking action, your response will lack authority and forcefulness. In situations that happen without warning, dualistic thought can mean disaster.

The average person believes he should think first then act. There is another saying more appropriate to emergencies: "He who hesitates is lost."

Every situation is not a matter of life and death, but if we learn to face the mother of all bad situations we can certainly deal with the minor scrimmages of day-to-day living.

Fear is the great enemy, the force which can grip the mind and paralyze us. On the path to developing a warrior's instinct we must replace fear with faith. Faith gives rise to the greatest power a warrior or anyone else could have—wisdom, also called instinctive wisdom. It is this power which was demonstrated by the samurai who faced ten armed swordsmen and won and by the Shaolin monks. It is the same power which works in ordinary people who affect amazing rescues or perform uncanny feats during emergencies. It is a power which lies hidden in you. But how do I know I have it? you may ask. You have it because you are a human being, and all those who have demonstrated these gifts are mere mortals such as you.

When two Masters cross swords or fight hand-to-hand, neither moves. Instead, they remain still . . . concentrated. If they are equally matched there will be no battle, for neither man will find a *suki*—a weakness—in his enemy. Weakness may simply be a flash of doubt in the mind. One moment of doubt is enough. The skilled attacker senses that flaw and attacks where his opponent feels most vulnerable. In the same manner, a career criminal senses those who have a victim mentality.

Students who probe the deepest meaning of the martial arts realize that the real enemy that must be defeated is oneself. Before you can begin to control a possible assailant, you must take control of your thoughts. A warrior must believe in his ability to win. If he cannot believe in himself, he is simply sacrificing his life when he enters a battle. To a defender, winning means surviving an assault. Before we explore the how-to, you must begin to believe that you can and will survive any violent or dangerous encounter because you will do what is necessary. To achieve this transformation of attitude you must begin to eliminate certain excess baggage which severely limits your activity. You need a change of perception. How you perceive yourself affects how you respond to danger.

A Mind Like Water

The mind of a child is vast and formless. It flows to whatever fascinates him or her at the moment. A child can concentrate on a game or a toy to the exclusion of all else. He has no mental conception of self so he is fully alive to the world around him rather than living through the tedium of his thoughts. Were it not for their lack of knowledge about the world they inhabit, children would be natural masters of Zen. Zen is that activity which flows unimpeded and without mediation from the Unconscious. It is action directed by instinctive wisdom rather than by ego or intellectual control—it is what we may call spiritual in origin. This mind is known by many names; one of them is the Unborn. Those who experienced this renewal of the mind were careful not to give us any concept by which we could pinpoint or "understand" it.

The Unborn, the mind like water, is real only to those who can experience it as a living reality. To attempt to grasp it as an intellectual concept is to murder it. Jesus Christ admonished his disciples to suffer little children to come unto him because the Kingdom of Heaven was open to those who approached it in the manner of little children. The Kingdom of Heaven, he later explained, is within us. We are back to the mind of childhood. What did you do to maintain your child mind when you still had your youthful innocence? How did you lose it?

To develop the instinct of the warrior, you must return to the childlike mind. By doing so you will lose none of your adult wisdom or knowledge, but you will be able to integrate intellectual understanding with nonverbal communication to regain oneness with your body. You will once again become alive to the world around you.

The Childlike Mind

We lose the virtue of the child mind as we gain greater dependence on spoken language and become more aware of the world. First the rules enforced by our parents and later the laws of society dictate how we should act and, in the process, how we should think. As a result of outside controls which are introduced by words and enforced by some type of threat, we begin to trust our own instincts less. We view our own direct impressions against outside demands and interpretations, creating a dualistic mind which divides the inner from the outer, me from you, in the larger sense good from evil, and so on. Authority becomes solidly associated with external forces, with words and symbols. Many of us lose that powerful sense of self-worth we felt as young children when we thought we could do anything. We begin to see ourselves more clearly through the eyes of our friends and associates and the world. In extreme cases, some of us feel like insignificant grains of sand in the endless universe. Nothing could be further from the truth.

Some people say that a young child thinks he is the center of the universe. In fact, the human being *is* the center of the universe, at least on Earth. All men, women, and children should recognize their value as living intelligences in our universe. Siddhartha Gotama, the ordinary man who later became known as the Buddha, reportedly said, "In the heavens above and the earth below, I alone am the most honored one." This claim would be a clear sign of a tremendous ego problem had he not also said that every man, woman, and child born were potentially buddhas, as well. In other words, whatever he discovered that transformed him into the Buddha is within all of us. Gotama uncovered the secret of who or what man is by looking within himself. When he did so, he found out that, all by himself, he was a being of great value. That means you too are a being of great value, since no human being can make a fundamental discovery about the nature of humankind that does not include all of us. Ostensibly, what is called Buddhism seeks to answer one essential question: "What is man?" The question is not an intellectual one to be satisfied by scientific study, but a spiritual one which can be satisfied only by penetrating insight which transforms the mind of the seeker, making him privy to a secret which cannot be shared with anyone except those who are in possession of that secret themselves. So what does all of this have to do with the warrior's instinct? You may find it interesting that all Asian martial arts can trace their roots back to discoveries about human nature made by either the Buddha or the inheritors of his insight. We learn from the Masters that the most vital teachings are not the most obvious ones. Your intuition is your greatest asset for this study, not your intellect. So we will be sharpening up your intuition.

It is not the role of society or our parents to teach us to look within ourselves for answers. They teach us to conform, to believe in the world we see as a fixed reality and they teach us how to succeed within the boundaries provided. We view the world with the aid of tools they have given us . . . once again, words and symbols. Our mind is reduced to words and responds to words. Unknown to most of us, we often respond to the symbol rather than reality. If we have been taught, for example, that members of a certain ethnic group are dangerous, we may react with fear when a member of that group gets on an elevator with us. We may be incapable of recognizing anyone of that race as an individual person and responding to his actions rather than to our misconceptions. An ethnic background becomes the automatic symbol for danger. This is push-button fear.

The warrior cannot afford the luxury of preconceptions. He or she must react only to what is actually happening . . . and that means he must remain focused in the *now*. Danger may come from a person or it may come from a situation. If a car comes speeding toward you out of control, it does not matter that this is something you never faced before; you must have the presence of mind to dart out of the way. There is no time to analyze or ask why the car is out of control. *Presence of mind.*

The young child is able to play with such concentration and learn with ease because his mind has no concept of past and future. He is *present*. Being present, he is full of energy. The child mind does not cling to things or events but drops them at will and moves on with equal intensity to whatever else he chooses to do. The Masters of old learned that this is the way of the Original Mind of man, nonclinging. When you cling to a fixed concept of yourself—doctor, janitor, lawyer or waitress, weak or strong—you develop a rigid program that your mind is compelled to support. It is not the duties that present a problem but our tendency to associate ourselves with a limited concept as self. It is this solid image of self that we fear will be harmed by an attacker. At the first sign of danger we cling protectively to our fixed image. But this image is no more the real you than a photograph is. The quicker you rid yourself of this crippling barrier, the more alive you will become to the moment and the endless variations of this remarkable creature called you.

A warrior must master his own responses. He

does not know what the enemy may do. He must be ready for anything. If your mind is solid like ice, you will be limited to preconceived or formula actions which may not fit the situations. If your mind is like water, it will adapt endlessly to the demand of the moment.

The car is speeding toward you . . . jump out of the way. Someone throws a fist at you . . . duck. What is complicated about that? The problem is that you may use the mind of thought but you don't understand the mind beyond thought. We will examine the power of no-thought later as it pertains to the Warrior Mind.

When I feared what a bully would do to me, I visualized that I was doomed to lose a confrontation. I thought of myself as weak. I won that first fight because all I thought about was that my father was looking. I loved my father and did not want him to think his son was a coward. When I was no longer thinking about the conceptual me, the real me was free to spring into action in a decisive manner. I won the day precisely because there was no thought of the powerless me. Suddenly there was strength and courage I had never experienced before.

Babies and young children are living beings, real persons, yet they have no ego-concept of who they are. Adults, on the other hand, erroneously believe that they cannot exist without a good healthy profile in their heads as guidelines for behavior. What they are doing is severely limiting themselves by this perception. It is like mistaking a ditch for the ocean. You are body, mind, and spirit. While we know the physical form is limited by nature, we cannot begin to measure the depth, width, and height of the mind and spirit. Why settle for less than the best you can muster from your person? From head to toe and through and through, you are a being of marvelous capabilities, filled with thrilling possibilities. You are the most astounding creature on Earth, the incredible human being. Animals have claws and horns, stings and fangs, but you have an incredible mind and a fathomless spirit. You need fear no man or beast, if you could only understand what you are.

To proceed we must agree that you are a human being. It does not matter what you do for a living, how much money you make, or how tall you are. All that matters is that you are a triune being made up of body, mind, and spirit. These are lessons for human beings based on the discovery, verified by all enlightened Masters and spiritual teachers through the ages, that mankind is one. If you can accept this common bond, that we are all humans, thus fundamentally the same, you will learn something that will not only make you more aware in this world of constant danger, but will also heighten your appreciation of the beauty of our kind as well.

The Principle: Shoshin: Restore Your Beginner's Mind

Long before you developed a concept to explain who you are, you were more fully alive and open to possibilities. Cease right now to dwell on these verbal barriers. Do not think of yourself in limiting terms such as doctor, lawyer, salesman, and such. These are functions of human beings, specialties. You are a human being, capable of far more than you suspect. Return to your beginner's mind (*shoshin*) as Zen Master Shunryu Suzuki calls it. It enables you to be open, to learn from anyone and everything. You studied your environment when you were a child because everything was brand-new. It must become new again. Every day is different no matter how routine it seems on the surface. This awareness is the foundation of a lifelong student. The warrior, no less than the scientist, is a student.

It is said that there is no head higher or lower than your own. In the universe all human beings have equal value; a scientist is not higher than a janitor. These are distinctions man makes for his own reasons. Begin right now to realize that all men, women, and children experience the nature of life as you do. They breathe, they eat, they feel, they think. Their lives is of equal value to yours. To believe in the value of your life is not enough. You must respect its presence in everyone, in everything. You must identify with the virtue of life, if you intend to be a defender of life. You must come to see that life is one. It lights up the bodies of all without exception . . . respect it in everyone and your own life will begin to take on universal dimensions.

A baby is the same whether it is born in China, Africa, or Europe. What direction his or her life takes after birth depends on environmental conditions and education; children are shaped by outside forces when they become old enough to understand.

14

A warrior cannot allow himself to be controlled by his environment. He adapts to his environment, learning to move within its limitations. There is but one thing the warrior must never lose control of—he must keep reign on his own mind.

We have all been conditioned by our upbringing; many of our responses to situations are not our own. If you desire to return the power to yourself, you must do as Zen Master Shunryu Suzuki once told his students: give your mind a thorough housecleaning. You must empty your mind. You may put some things back, if you feel you need them, but it is important to get a fresh mental start. For example, just because people point to a place above their head as "up" is no reason that you should attach to their concept as absolute. The Earth is hanging in empty space. We are surrounded by "up." Realizing that, you may still go back to the original concept for convenience sake but now a little wiser. We must practice this mind-cleaning, that is, getting beyond limitations which are the product solely of the way we use and misuse the mind. The samurai counted his mind as his friend. Before you can do the same, some housecleaning is absolutely necessary.

Practice: Shinsai: Mind Fasting

You may be accustomed to increasing your knowledge by reading newspapers or books, watching television, or engaging in stimulating intellectual conversations with the wife, husband, or friends. You may find it exciting pitting your intellect against others'. For a while, however, your *sensei* would like you to practice a more passive role. I want your mind to become feminine in the classical sense of yielding, receptive, nonaggressive. Do not dwell on what you know. Instead, I want you to realize how little you know. Concentrate not on your fullness but your emptiness. If you are full, you are satisfied. If you are empty, there is hunger that craves to be satiated. With this feeling of mental poverty, take a walk.

As you see the trees, look at them as individual life forms; see their uniqueness, the curve of a branch, the flaw in a leaf. Do not see them in the shorthand code of the word "tree." Look at them as if there was no word for them and you had never seen one before. It is likely that you haven't really *seen* a tree since your childhood. With the same state of mind, listen to birds without calling them robins or sparrows. See, hear, feel—do not talk to yourself about what you are seeing, hearing, and feeling. Let your mind observe and react but ignore your tendency to comment in words. Let the words pass. In this manner, experience people and events as you walk along, see and hear them as unique expressions of life and form.

To train your mind and reduce the words which try to overpower you, here is a useful technique.

The Breath

There is a link between the breath and consciousness noted by all enlightened teachers. That awareness was not lost on Master warriors. To calm your mind and give you a point of focus, count your exhalations from one to ten. When you reach ten, start back at one again. Sounds easy, doesn't it? But be forewarned—you will lose count. When you do, go back to one. This simple exercise will increase your concentration and divert your attention from random thoughts. Do not strain your breathing. Follow your natural breaths. Your breathing will become deeper without your conscious effort.

Do this exercise while you walk, whether it is in a mall or on the city streets. It is my version of the *kinhin* (walking meditation) exercise taught by Zen Masters. Avoid conversations while you are practicing; if you are cornered, be brief and move on. Remember—you are a student of the Master warriors. You are forging your sword . . . the sword is your very own mind . . . it is wielded effectively only through awareness.

Remember that you are practicing awareness without the clutter of verbal thought, so, as words come, let them pass without elaboration.

You may be asking where is the action. How can all this help me fight for my life? Ever heard the phrase "mind over matter"? You have a body—that is matter. You have a mind. If you control your mind, it will in turn control your body. Although the body and mind are not one, they are so interwoven as to function as one when balance is restored. The mind is the sword, but it is the body which holds it. The body does not guide the sword . . . the sword should control the movement of the body.

What is he saying? you ask. This is a job for your intuition. Practice, practice the principles as presented here and all will become clear in time. The *sensei* throws the punch. You have to block, yourself. The goal is well worth the effort.

MAKE YOUR MIND
YOUR FRIEND AND HERO

The warriors of old were virtually alone in battle. Each man or woman had to employ his or her skill against one or more opponents. There was no high-tech equipment on which to rely; they depended on their own senses and skill to get them out of situations. The Master warrior learned to make his own mind his friend. One would think that everyone's mind would have his best interest at heart but such is not the case. If we think of the mind as our own onboard computer, we must also be aware that it acts according to its programming. Clearly, all of our early education or programming came from outsiders. Our view of the world and our thoughts about other people were given to us by our parents, teachers, ministers, and the like. Even though we become more aware of what enters our minds as we grow older, we continue to respond to impressions previously planted. Unfortunately, those who impressed

their views upon us also gave us their fears and prej-
udices with which to contend, as well. It is highly
likely that your mind, as is, is not altogether your best
friend. In many ways it could be subtly working
against you. For that reason, as we have noted, it is
important to start fresh and return to a beginner's
mind. A true Master is keenly aware that he knows
nothing. He clings to no concept or words about
things. He experiences and lets go, trusting his mind
to absorb what is important much as the ocean
receives raindrops. Each raindrop becomes part of
the ocean without disturbing or altering its essence.

To make the mind your friend, you must free it
to follow its own nature. That means you must cease
to think of the mind as an actual object that can be
adequately defined and conceptualized. That which
is programmed and controlled is more accurately
labeled the ego. The ego is that narrow perception of
self we can visualize or identify in words. As the
raindrop is water but not the ocean, the ego is an
aspect of mind but not the true mind. The true mind
can no more be bound by words than can the
Creator. For the mind to be your friend you must
have the courage to allow it to be true to its real
nature. The Chinese Masters were direct: *Hsin Hsin
Ming*—have faith in your mind. The very word
"faith" suggests letting go, trusting something or
someone to act in your behalf . . . but can the mind
act without your conscious manipulation? It does so
every day of your life.

Your Friendly Mind at Work

When you desire to walk, you walk. Your legs move by a silent, imperceptible command we call *will*. When you sleep, you breathe through the night without having to stay awake to make sure that the process takes place. You digest your food without direct supervision and both see and hear without having to make special effort. In many ways, your mind is functioning without the necessity of your conscious awareness. If you have faith in your mind, you will allow it to work.

The Principle

A Shogun once challenged his retainers to strike his pet monkey, who was poised on his lap. No matter how fast the warriors were, they could not get near the animal. When Zen Master Takuan entered, he was invited to try. In short order, the Master accomplished the goal. When asked how he alone succeeded, Takuan said, "When the others struck, they were worried about striking your lap," he said to the Shogun. "I did not worry about hitting you but focused fully on striking the monkey." Takuan demonstrated what happens when the mind is allowed to act without interference or deliberation. The retainers attempted to monitor their actions out of fear of failure. As a result they failed. The mind must be free to act on its own. Any attempt to govern the outcome in the midst of action is to raise the specter of the double mind once again.

To develop our natural ability to act sponta-
neously and appropriately to situations, we must
improve our relationship with our mind. We must
reach the point where we trust it to respond as necessary. To develop that confidence we must prove
that our mind does, in fact, possess marvelous ability. After all, the same mind that moves our arms and
legs and processes information so that we can talk at
will is the same one that can move us out of the path
of danger or provide us with a means of escape in an
emergency. This kind of ability emerges from a calm,
serene mind, not from a state of panic. Everyone's
mind is capable of marvelous activity, but only if it is
allowed to *be*. Often we have heard people say, "I
should have followed my first mind." That statement
suggests that the person engaged a second mind
instead. Zen Master Bankei warned against the
reliance on second thoughts. He admonished his disciples to consider the second thought as powerless to
influence them.

To your practice of watching the breath add
another practice. The *sensei* wants you to practice
disregarding second thoughts. Forcefully go with
your first thoughts, whether you're choosing a movie
or dinner or are about to answer a question. You
must overcome the feeling that your second thought
is better just because it is second. The purpose of this
exercise is to eliminate avenues of hesitation. Once
you go to the second thought, it is easy to retreat to
more thoughts. You soon find yourself trapped in
indecision. Once cluttered with thoughts, your mind
inhibits your ability to act. Fluid action comes from a

fluid mind. As urban warrior you must enjoy a fluid mind. This is the mind that will be your friend in any situation.

The Street Fight

In a real-life situation, I was attacked by four street fighters who were out to prove that the martial arts were useless against them. In only moments, I countered their assault and threw the men one by one to the ground. Onlookers were very impressed with my ability, but to me it was easier than fighting one person. As they attacked, my body flowed naturally from one position to another. I was not conscious of thought until after the fight was over. This is the value of a fluid mind . . . *mushin* (no mind). Remember, the body moves without the need of verbal command. The tendency we have to guide ourselves through a physical crisis verbally prevents action. Had I dwelt on the number of men attacking me, or how I would deal with them, I would have been psychologically overwhelmed by their number. Experience had proven to me that the inner man knew exactly what to do, so I remained relaxed. My thoughts were expressed as actions, not words. There was no running commentary in my mind, just one motion after another.

Once again we should contemplate the child mind. Babies and young children act. Their minds are expressed as action, not words, whereas as adults we tend to focus on the mind as words. With practice we can come to see that our mental life is far richer than that. For now, practice disregarding the second thought when it comes to action or speech. Act with confidence from your first mind . . . the original impulse. Give yourself permission to make a mistake. It is human to err. If you continue to practice you will unconsciously begin to discern the sure path. When a typist taps the keys of a typewriter with confidence without looking at the keyboard, his or her fingers zip along correctly, but let that person have a moment of doubt or suddenly have the desire to look, and suddenly the work becomes halting and unsure. Let your mind work and find its own way without interference. We have been taught that we must control the mind—but how? Zen Master Shunryu Suzuki said we should control cattle by giving them a huge meadow. Control the mind by giving it huge freedom in which to operate.

The beautiful thing about these mental exercises is that you can practice everywhere. The world is your *dojo* (school). Do the exercises well and you will notice greater unity between mind and body. The mind should be master of the body . . . mind over matter, not the other way around. An uncertain mind is not a good master. By the time you work your way through these lessons, you will discover that your mind is more awesome than you ever dreamed, but still it is not your most inspiring feature. There is much more to you than you currently understand and far more to the Warrior Mind than just fighting.

Again, as you practice going with your first mind in decision-making, be willing to be wrong for the sake of fluidity and spontaneity. There is a saying, "The conflict between good and evil [read right and wrong] is the disease of the mind." Eliminate the fear of error, and you have come a long way toward experiencing a renewed mind. Relax—your innate sense of correctness is always with you. It does not need your conscious observance to keep you from violating your moral code or finding the proper path of action.

Our study is a path of unlearning. Before you can find the way you must first give up your false perceptions. An error the size of a hair will send you careening off course. Such is the sensitive nature of this thing we call *mind*.

ONENESS

When you think of yourself, what do you mean? Are you referring to body or mind or spirit . . . or do you know? We are accustomed to dividing ourselves in language, but in life no such division is possible. Before children are given tools of a verbal language, they have a holistic perception of self. We are not just fingers and hands, a head, torso, and various other parts. We are the whole person. As we become accustomed to thinking of ourselves as various parts, we also find ourselves exerting conscious effort to control them. The Master warrior learned to employ his sword, bow, or spear as an extension of his body. The weapon became one with the body. Thus the implication is that he perceived his body as one. How do we achieve this unity of being?

Division is a function of the mind. It is in the mind that the division becomes "real" and it is through renewal of our mind that we can overcome its power to impede our use of our body. In the book

Zen and the Art of Archery, Eugene Herrigal discovers through the art of Zen archery that he was able to shoot an arrow without exerting conscious control over the bow or his body. Speaking of the act, he wrote, "It shot." Who is this It that shot? When the ego, the conceptual you, is absent, then It manifests. We will not make the mistake of creating a concept to describe what this seemingly mystical It is, but I suggest that when body, mind, and spirit are in unity, the ego or conceptual self diminishes in power and that which acts is free of the usual past baggage. It freely acts based on the needs of the moment. This active power we are calling It arises only in the present moment. However, although It acts in the present moment, all that you have experienced and learned in life is accessible but without deliberation. By use of the word "It," I do not imply some "other" power which operates in your place. On the contrary, It is none other than your original nature, that which defies definition. Faith is needed to experience this level of being and activity. As Shunryu Suzuki-Roshi taught his students, it is absolutely necessary to believe in Nothing. This is not the nothing which is the opposite of the word "something." It is faith in *that which cannot be apprehended by senses.* This is in keeping with the teaching of the Bible: "He who is within you is greater than he who is in the world." The "He" mentioned cannot be seen by x-ray or found by any external physical instrument, including the eyes. To trust the superior "He" within you, you must effectively surrender your conscious control to this undiscernible presence . . . leaving your mind with no image or concept to grasp. The Lord in His primordial identity is formless and utterly beyond conception. Man as a creature in His image must contain similar attributes to be worthy of the comparison. The fallen Adam (man) is mind-conscious or conscious of a self which carries over from day to day like the body. In the enlightened man only He exists. There is no personal self that can be found to exist in the body. Who are we without the experiences and memories we have made in our body? We move, breathe, and have our being. We have nothing to do with our ability to do these things. It is our nature. The warrior and the sage both learn to trust this Unborn nature. It is called Unborn because, unlike the body which had to come into the world, the Unborn, the "He" of the Bible, was here from the beginning. The sage and the warrior come to the same conclusion in time. Human mastery comes only when a man can deny the world of the senses, the logic of the seen, and experience the reality of life from a place beyond body-mind. When body and mind are "sacrificed," brought into submission, the Light which lighteth all men stands in its glory. Those who follow this path, whether they are artist, warrior, or minister by vocation, discover that there is a living intelligence within, which has the power to move independently of the mind. It is vastly superior.

The warrior is a student of the Self. He discovers the breadth and depth of his powers as a man by facing the *koan* of battle. As a Zen koan challenges the intellect by presenting a question that is beyond its power to answer, so does battle present a situation that must be answered not with thought but with precise and appropriate action . . . wisdom. Wisdom manifests when the intellect yields.

The Keys of Success

As you can imagine, when you expound on super-awareness of the Warrior Mind, people often test you when you least expect it. The key factor in super-awareness afforded by the Warrior Mind is that one should expect something to happen at any time. The warrior knows that the only time in which things can happen is now. He or she must be aware right now. The sages taught that one should walk as if on thin ice. The samurai entered a room as if the ceiling could fall at any moment. Indeed, it could. Danger or accidents usually occur when we are not ready for them. Be alert all the time. The *sensei* does not mean for you to become paranoid. Make it a game you play with yourself. If you were playing handball you would move with amazing speed and agility to return the ball on the rebound. If you were playing dodge ball, you would try not to be hit. In your daily life you must learn to see, hear, feel, smell, and sense your environment as you work and play. You must make greater use of the senses you take for granted and the ones you don't even know you have. Like the animals of the jungle and fish of the sea, human beings have natural enemies, mostly other humans. Our newspapers give daily testimony to this fact. Do not be deceived by the advance of technology; the world is still a jungle in many ways. We would be wise to accept this reality and adapt our attitude accordingly.

One afternoon, I was giving a talk on self-defense and awareness to security guards at a New York hotel. Unbeknownst to me, one of the men doubted my ability to live up to my words. Without warning he threw a ring filled with keys straight for my face. Without hesitation, my hand snatched them from the air before they could strike me. I placed the jangling keys on the desk behind me and continued talking. Later, I publicly reprimanded the officer for risking my well-being with the prank. "Suppose I had failed. You would have proven your point by hurting me," I said. Secretly, however, I was glad he gave me the opportunity to show that I can do what I preach.

As the guard prepared to throw the keys, I felt an inner signal that alerted me that I was in danger. Instantly, my eyes scanned the room. By the time the keys were in the air, my body was ready to do what was necessary to avoid harm. None of my actions were controlled by a conscious decisions. If I had thought out my movements, I would have been struck.

The power of cultivating the Warrior Mind lies in awakening the ability to act unconsciously . . . from *mushin* . . . a state of No Mind, as Zen Masters call it. *Mushin* is not really the absence of mind but rather a mind that functions with the clarity of a mirror. As a mirror reflects objects without clinging to the images so that it can reflect one object after another without being stained by them, so can your mind respond and let go, free to flow to the next situation without impediment. How do we do this?

The way you are sitting right now expresses your state of mind and tells how you perceive yourself. The way you walk or stand does the same. Have you ever watched a person enter a room who exuded power and grace? Have you ever watched a tiger move? Powerful statements are made without a word being spoken. Countenance is an instrument of a warrior. If your posture is good you may never have to fight. Posture is the outer expression on an inner state. If you can learn to control your posture—walking, sitting, lying, and standing—you will have discovered an effective tool for fine-tuning your mind. Remember, body and mind are neither two nor one, but they complement each other so well that you can train your mind through working on the body and vice versa.

The yogis are well aware of the power of posture. They have made a full study of it. The statues of various buddhas and other enlightened Masters show them in various *asanas* (postures). Their bodies radiate power, serenity, and even love. Noticeable also are the graceful poses of the *mudra* (hand). Hands also reflect our inner state. How we use them can affect the way we react to different stimuli. So how can posture help you develop the Warrior Mind?

The movie *Red Sun* pitted an American cowboy played by Steve McQueen against a samurai played by Toshiro Mifune. Most impressive about the samurai was the way he moved. His back was always straight and he performed every task with concentration and grace. His demeanor was one of stillness, like the calmness of the sky which gives no hint of the

31

lightning bolt to come. There was power and control suggested by each movement of Mifune's body. His body was responsive to his will. He was beautiful and awesome to watch. Although the samurai of Mifune was small in stature, he commanded the screen like a giant.

Shi Sei Practice

All that we see of you is your form. Before you open your mouth, we have already seen what you think and feel about yourself. It shows in your movement, in your countenance. It is punctuated by the gestures of your hand. The famous statue *The Thinker* by Rodin clearly reveals the activity of the subject without our having to know the title of the work. The pose of the man shouts loudly that he is in deep thought. If you are distracted when you walk down a street or approach your car, your body will reveal that truth to the alert criminal looking for a victim. Like the samurai of Toshiro Mifune, you must learn to project the dynamic energy of readiness and awareness through your body. Only a fool would think he could sneak up on a resting tiger. Its body language warns that the big cat never sleeps, if sleeping is meant to mean unconsciousness. Like the cat, you can learn to be always "on" even when you are in a deep state of rest. This is possible because you will be using that part of Self that is always conscious anyway. The Bible states, "He who is within you is greater than he who is in the world." The implication is that the greater part of our life is not that which is apparent to the senses. Since we are told that this "He" is within us it should be obvious that to experience this truth we must turn inward. Since He is greater than our mind or body, those parts which are in the world, we must willingly surrender our limited understanding in order to receive direction from within. This "He" is the Master, equally reflected within the pool of all human life but not equally perceived. He is the art of the artists, the wisdom of the sage, the skill of the warrior. He is the unseen model for all that is graceful and beautiful, the sweetness in honey. To the degree that we are able to follow the Way as it is revealed within us, to that degree do we master any skill, art, or discipline. Man is in the likeness of God, and therefore can emulate His nature in various ways. Since God can act instantly without need of deliberation, so can we under certain circumstances. Great warriors, both those formally trained in Zen and those who have intuitively found the inner path, have noted that in moments of great need something other than their conscious selves has delivered them in battle. They are able to fight with a skill superior to their training and act with serenity, grace, and detachment. The Zen phrase *Mushin No Shin* is often translated as "No Mind." It connotes that state of acting with instinctive wisdom which precludes conscious thought. This ability is not something that a man achieves by some act on his part. It happens when he reaches a state of rest and allows the experience to manifest. This brings us back to faith. Life is a mystery and we are inseparable from the mystery. If you think you know everything about what you are, this book will not be of service to you. If, on the other hand, you know that there is more to all of us than is easily seen, you can open the door to exciting discoveries about yourself. So where does posture fit in?

The fashion model is adept at projecting with just her form and expressions the desired moods suggested by the photographer. Concentrate on an animal you think to be powerful. Feel that power. Now express that feeling through your body. If you chose a tiger, for example, imagine that you are that tiger in human form. You are the creature which commands respect from all the other denizens of the jungle. You power comes from within you. You do not need approval from the outside to feel strong. Stand with the assurance of your power. Walk with it. You are the tiger. To do this exercise effectively you must not focus on the picture of your chosen animal (model) in your mind, nor think about its attributes in words. You must express it through bodily actions. When you were a child you did this kind of role playing often. Bring that enthusiasm to this practice and you will experience how the body can be used to change the mental states to your advantage.

Many martial arts can be directly traced to the study of animals. The beautiful white crane inspired White Crane Kung Fu. There is another form of Kung Fu which owes its origin to an insect. Praying Mantis Kung Fu was derived from movements of its namesake. There are martial arts movements based on the mythological actions of the dragon, such as devastating kicks patterned after the lashing tail of the creature of Chinese lore. It is thought that the famous Kung Fu style now known as Shaolin originated from the eighteen movements of Lo Han. The Buddhist patriarch Bodhidharma was inspired to develop a defensive arts from the movements of animals after meditating on the need for self-protection on his journey from India to China. Thus a man of peace founded a great warrior art based on a peaceful and natural approach. By emulating the *spirit* (as in approach) of your animal model you are able to nonverbally gain the feel of your potential power, agility, and grace without verbal blocking.

When you are frightened by something you may tremble. Trembling is an expression of your mind. Just as easily you can respond to the frightening stimuli by clenching your fist and taking an on-guard stance. This too is an expression of your mind. To be a warrior you must express your mind through your bodily actions without hesitation. There must be no hesitation between thought, action, and reaction. As a famous Zen analogy explains, when flint strikes steel there is a spark. Zen is that response . . . it simply happens. That is the life-saving way of the warrior.

Knowledge can be traced to its source, but wisdom comes out of *no thing* and *no where* we can pinpoint. Even if we say wisdom comes from God we are saying the same thing because God is beyond definition. The warrior is a person of action. He or she values superior action. In a life-and-death situation, action must come before words. The warrior can abandon his life to the caprice of the unknown because he has learned to rely on wisdom, not knowledge. Although he does not understand the how and why of wisdom, he knows it has no second. Wisdom guides his body. His mind remains . . . the observer. After the action, the intellect may analyze and comment—but not before.

Your body is an expression of force in form—*Shi Sei*, in Japanese. The *hi* (form) is present in the word *Bushido*, "The Way of the Warrior." What *Bushido* suggests is that the Way of the Warrior is to cease the struggle (*Bu*). The warrior discovers the secret of martial arts only when he ceases the war in his mind. This act ends the conflict between me and you. When there is no one to be perceived as the enemy, conflict within the warrior ceases. This is a wonderful experience because when the conflict disappears, the warrior is able to recognize legitimate threats from the outside while living with an attitude of peace.

In order for us to experience the wisdom which can guide our bodies and reveal ourselves to us in action, we must opt for action over our own words. While the Word of God is living power, we fool ourselves if we attribute this same power to our own words. Our actions speak louder than our words, as one astute thinker noted, but God's words are active. Action alone is proof of the veracity of our understanding . . . but to understand we must change the balance in our lives.

AIR SPACE:
THE WINGSPAN THEORY

By right of birth we are all entitled to breathing space of our own. I call this concept of movable breathing space the Wingspan Theory. In order to take flight, a bird must have enough space to stretch his wings. As a young man, I felt that I had the right to a circle of peace I could call my own. The space from fingertip to fingertip as I stretched out my arms and described a circle in the air, including above my head, I called my Wingspan. This was my personal air space to protect. The world could be in turmoil, but I wanted to maintain peace and serenity within my own Wingspan. I respected the right of others to preserve their own territory. Wherever I would go from day to day I carried the sense of freedom that was my own Wingspan.

By limiting my sense of personal space to the length and depth of my outstretched arms, my area of concentration was small and manageable. I learned to sense that space as an invisible globe surrounding my body. No one has the right to do harm to us. The Wingspan Theory reenforces the sense that your body is yours to guard from any outside threat. It trains the senses on the outer perimeter of your body so that you become sensitive to anything that would threaten your well-being, not just persons but protruding objects such as a branch jutting from a tree or a skate left in the hallway. The Wingspan approach to defense trains you to focus your awareness in a field that radiates outward from your person into the world around you. This training produces spontaneous results. How you respond to stimuli depends on your learning to trust your responses to the wisdom of No Mind—that is, the instinctive wisdom we have already discussed.

Practicing Wingspan

In a standing position, stretch your arms out to the side and close your eyes. Concentrate on your body. Feel that you are sensing the air around you and above your head. Turn around slowly, sensing the air as you complete a circle. Stretch your arms in front of you, then slowly thrust them above your head. Bring them down to the outstretched position again and pull them back as far as you can, as if you were using them as wings.

After developing a sense of your own Wingspan, you need to practice throwing punches and executing blocks within that space. In slow motion and fully focused on your outgoing breath, throw a punch toward an imaginary opponent. Practice blocking blows in slow motion as well. Techniques can be added and refined through daily or periodic practice. These exercises are meant to teach the unconscious that it should strike back and defend against assault. This teaching is accomplished by demonstrating proper response to stimuli, not by words. In the martial arts, the performance of *kata* gives the student a catalogue of techniques to draw upon in a battle. Whether you use boxing, streetfighting, or martial arts techniques is not important. What is important is not only that you give yourself permission to protect yourself but also that you "program" yourself with some techniques to draw upon. The Warrior Mind is capable of adapting and expanding on techniques as necessary once it harmonizes with the body. A blow is swung, and ducking or blocking is the natural response. If there is no hesitation between thought and action, no breakdown between what the mind perceives and what the body does, then you are safely moved out of harm's way. The body must yield to the mind as a rose petal to the wind. In the highest art even the mind yields, but only to the fathomless depth of the spirit. When you are conscious of blocking and striking, then your body is moving in oneness with mind. When the blocks and counterblows come without thought or effort, your activity is said to be spiritual, thus of No Mind. The Zen Masters say that only when you have no mind in things and no thing in mind can your action be marvelous, empty and free. To experience that kind of response to danger is beautiful and humbling. It points to that innermost nature of our being which lies beyond intellect and explanation. Such actions are said to come from emptiness because there is no traceable source for its wondrous activity.

The Warrior's Path is one of action. It is a good metaphor for the journey of life. At any given time we could be called upon to make a life-or-death decision, whether in a fight or when simply driving in heavy traffic. When one faces the possibility of death at any moment, life itself becomes more intensified. Flowers seem more beautiful, the sunrise is more awesome. Too often we take life for granted, and therefore we lose our appreciation for the simple things of day-to-day life. The warrior is keenly aware that the next moment is not guaranteed. Forced to look at time as a precious commodity, the warrior is able to appreciate seconds as well as days and weeks. This consciousness shift awakens the creative sensitivity that produces the soul of the artist. The artist, like the warrior, must capture the essence of life as it flashes past or lose it forever.

Wingspan reminds us that our bodies are mortal. They can be easily hurt, even by accident, so we must remain aware in order to protect them from harm. It also heightens our sense of pleasure. Our hearing becomes keener, our sense of smell becomes more sensitive, and even our ability to feel life through the very pores of our skin is enhanced by this constant attention. Our sense of life is heightened by our newfound sensitivity to our surroundings. Practice and you will discover ever more exciting things about the person called you as you interact with the environment at large. Although the Wingspan approach was something that I developed from my own meditation, I recognize it as just another name for the path discovered by the Ch'an and Zen Masters of old. It is a nonverbal training method for confronting life in its raw suchness. If we are to become men and women of action, we must dive from our carefully constructed platform of words to into the empty air. If the air can support us, we will fly. If not, we will crash to the ground. Only those who take the plunge experience the truth. The others die a little day by day. The Master is within you, but you will never make contact until you demonstrate the courage it takes to rely on Him.

Beneath the doubting mass of the ego is the great warrior of life who can meet any challenge. He is the One in All, the All in One. He cannot be seen with the naked eyes, He cannot be found through philosophy or religion; but the man or woman who returns to the trusting mind of childhood radiates His power all day long, but knows not how.

THE WAY IS VOID,
THE ORIGINAL MIND

Master Yagyu Munnenori, author of *The Book of Family Traditions on the Art of War,* said, "If you accord with original mind, you will excel in martial arts." In fact, you will excel in any art or endeavor. Whether we use the term No Mind, *Mushin,* Everyday Mind or Original Mind, we are pointing to the same truth: self-mastery, whether as a warrior or an artisan, begins with returning to one's proper mental roots. Activity which flows from the Original Mind is direct and flawless. Those with eyes to see will recognize the movements of a Master. The Original Mind is not something you must cultivate. It existed before even your parents were born. Your body came into the world but the Original Mind was here already. It functions within you daily but is counteracted by the false mind we have been taught to project in its place. The Original Mind is called void because it cannot be seen. When it is still we call it void; when it moves we call it mind. It manifests in the movement of our hands and feet or in the hands and feet of your opponent. Until it manifests in movement, it is void or empty . . . mysterious. Like the enlightened Masters of the Himalayas as well as of China and Japan, Munnenori notes that the Original Mind in us is the mind of the universe. Its movement manifests as thunder, lightning, and rain. It is this Mind which walks and talks and is our individual selves. This is not a philosophy to be discussed and marvelled at but the actual experience of those who let themselves drop back into the void of their being. This is the home that the first man, Adam, abandoned in pursuit of intellectual or secondary knowledge. It was not a good trade.

Returning to the Original Mind heals the split in the mind. It eradicates duality. When duality is gone there is no sense of a me facing a world or the defender against the attacker. There is wholeness. Responses are appropriate to the given situation but not forced. When the sun shines, darkness flees of its own accord; just as easily, it reappears when the light recedes. In truth, the world, you, and your antagonist are all living in the void together. The separation is apparent only to the eyes. Just as the Original Mind orchestrates the dance of the universe, it can move your body in perfect accord to the circumstances of life, if you stop interfering by the power of the false mind. Your false mind is constructed of erroneous views and the habit of clinging to past events and notions. Clinging to these memories may give people the sense of continuity, but it is in fact a way of draining the dynamic energy from life which is at its best when it is one electric spark after another giving rise to new energy and experiences moment after moment. The void is oneness. Where there is oneness there is appropriate action without the sense of there being a person apart from the act that is making it happen. Everyone has at one time or another moved unexplainably to catch a falling object with agility and grace but also without effort. If you have ever experienced such a response to a situation, you have tasted the kind of normal activity that arises out of the Original Mind.

The Warrior Mind is the Original Mind functioning in the realm of self-defense. It is possible to experience the Original Mind in the practice of a certain art but not during everyday activity. It takes vigilance to realize the Original Mind in whatever you do. To reach this state is to reach the height of Zen Masters and Himalayan yogis. With specialized awareness you can master various arts. This point was illustrated when a samurai swordsman was beaten by a young man who insisted he fight with a wooden sword used for practice bouts. The Master lost. Later when he was in a fight against six men armed with real swords he won within seconds and killed them all. When the young warrior saw this he was amazed. "How did I defeat a man with such great skill?" he asked. "You had a wooden sword," the Master said. The old Master knew how to use the Original Mind in a battle to the death, but he was caught in a net of thoughts when he had to do battle according to the rules of sportsmanship.

Raising the Original Mind is a matter of letting it be. The Bible says, "Let this mind be in you which was in Christ Jesus . . ." The word "let" suggests that this mind is already present in you. The Bible goes on to refer to that mind as oneness with God. This is the incredible mind of which we speak. It is accessible to everyone but experienced by only a few. Consider again what the Enlightened One known as the Buddha was reported to have said: "In the heavens above and the earth below, I alone am the most honored one." This experience is further confirmation of Original Mind. The Buddha is declaring that there is nothing else present in the universe but his all-encompassing mind. Yet, the Buddha also declares that all sentient beings, even you, are none other than Buddha.

Direct experience is irrefutable truth. The warrior seeks to embrace the power of his being. Although the path may be obscured by the language of religion, the warrior practices the teachings to experience the virtue of the Way as reality. The Way is a science disguised in religious code. The Western mind is prone to search out truth through the tangible, the seen. The Light of Asia illuminates the void. It starts where nothing has yet been created. Although the intellect has nothing which to lay hold of and no words can adequately convey what is indicated, it precipitates a living transformation of being which evokes power and wisdom. For the first time, one understands what a human being is. For the first time, one is capable of being fully human. This is not a moment for bragging or exaltation. One is humbled and grateful. At this point you realize you can no more lay claim to your ability than lay claim to hanging the stars in the heavens. The marvelous mystery is crystal clear, yet now you understand that the mere wiggling of your finger is proof of the supernatural origin of the universe. In fact, the supernatural and the ordinary are different names for the same experience.

As a student of the Warrior Mind, realize now that the power is all on your side despite the threats of the enemy. The outcome is yours to dictate. You can take his sword from his hands before he blinks or disarm him with the speed of thought. You can take away his fighting spirit with a spoken word. You can do all these things and more because the battle, the contest, is not in the world you think you see before you but takes place solely in the void, in the mind that links him to you and you to him. You are the roaring lion and the soaring eagle because you think you are and for no other reason. Practice this attitude. Prove to yourself that it is so.

Everyday Practice

During the course of a day many events occur. Some are expected, others are not. On our jobs we must perform routine tasks and meet emergencies when necessary. Let us say that those occurrences we expect fall within the realm of the known, or the realm of form. We see what is happening and we meet it. The unknown or unexpected occurs in emptiness. It is like seeing the furniture in the room without appreciating the hollow space in which we move. Come to realize that this invisible essence, this empty space, is as much a part of your life and mind as all you see. Your sense of self cannot be whole if all you are aware of is form. The universal mind is form. But the universal mind is also emptiness. Form is also emptiness and emptiness is also form. Zen Masters tell us this so that we can let go of both form and emptiness as something we must cling to. Letting go, we see that the cup in our hands still appears solid and the wind still cannot be seen or held by the fingers. A Zen poem illustrates this principle.

Before I studied Zen,
mountains were mountains and rivers were rivers.
After I had studied for a while,
mountains were no longer mountains and rivers
were no longer rivers.
After I mastered Zen,
mountains were once again mountains
                              and rivers once again rivers.

The field of practice is your everyday life. It is there that you will experience the Zen of the Warrior Mind at work, even if you are never called upon to actually fight an opponent. When you drink your coffee as if it is the most important act in the world, savoring the flavor as it flows over your tongue, you are practicing. When you interface with your computer as if it were your antagonist ready to lop off your head with his gleaming sword, you will be keenly alert and focused. When you observe people, places, and things as if this is the last moment you will have with them you teach yourself to live in the vital moment . . . your pores are alive to life around you.

As your day unfolds, do not retreat to the past and review today as just a repeat of last week or some other time. Today has never happened before even though the environment is familiar. You do not know what the next second will bring. The duties of your work may involve planning, but remain open to emptiness, to the Original Mind for creative input at any time. Now the day is no longer routine. It is an adventure at every turn. A walk to the water cooler could yield unexpected excitement or trigger an exciting turn of events. As you tap into the dynamic field of the universal mind, you spark responses in kind from those around you, even though they may not be consciously aware of what is happening. If it rains, a man sleeping on a park bench will still get wet, even if he is unaware of the sensation.

We live in the information age. We think that the more we consciously understand the better we will be able to perform. There is indeed a need for specialized knowledge, but the way to master it and ourselves is not to stay self-consciously aware of how we acquired the information but to let go of it. We must learn to trust the Original Mind to synthesize and use these facts and figures in the way most appropriate to our needs. Whether we think or act fast or slowly it is still we—ourselves—who are making the decision to act. Only when the false mind is eliminated can we defeat the sense that there is another road within us to take. There is only the real you, complete in every way, and the false, fragmented self which doubts the instinctive wisdom inherent in your being.

As we learn to flow into the affairs of the day, meeting the rising and falling circumstances as they come, we will learn how the body accommodates itself to the revelations of Original Mind. We will learn to trust our true selves once again.

The Warrior Mind must be calm and peaceful. The conflict must not exist within him. When he is hungry the warrior will eat; when he is thirsty he will drink. If he is inspired he will write a poem or play music. When attacked he will defend. The mind that eats and drinks, writes and plays a musical instrument is the same mind that defends. Form changes to accommodate function. One moment the arm is extended to shake a hand, the next it is extended to block a blow.

If defense is your objective you do not harbor the desire to either experience or cause bodily harm but to maintain the peace. Peace and salvation is what you offer, a way out with dignity and tact. When you are clear on your purpose the Original Mind will create the means by which you may accomplish this.

Osensei Morihei Uyeshiba, founder of Aikido, declared that the true purpose of the martial way was love, "to receive the spirit of the universe and spread his peace." Aikidoists learn to defend themselves with that spirit of peace as their source of power. Aikido is notable for its serenity, grace, and power.

Learn to radiate the *ki* (spirit) of peace and love silently as you move through your day. You accomplish this simply by exerting your will in that direction. You want your co-workers and even strangers to feel that you are a vessel of love and peace. As you do this exercise you will be transforming yourself into just that, cultivating *te* (virtue) that will be there if you are ever called upon to defend that peace. By performing this quiet exercise daily you will be creating a Wingspan of peace and love. This, in itself, will serve to ward off all but the most hardened antagonists.

The scripture says, "For as a man thinketh so is he." If you think peace and love you will surely be the vessel of peace and love. People will respond to you in more positive ways unconsciously because they will feel the attractiveness of your spirit.

Practice this refining of your energy in the ordinary affairs of day-to-day life. Daily life is the battlefield. Make your ordinary use of body your *kata*, your demonstration of form. You are universal mind expressed as man. What is your body telling us about you? Become aware of form. Become sensitive to the movement of your body as you go from task to task. You want your body to flow with your mind, not against it.

SHIKANTAZA:
THE POWER OF JUST SITTING

I entered the Warrior Path for two reasons. I was the target of bullies daily and Southern Black men were an endangered species. I read about senseless lynching by racists who seemed to commit their crimes against humanity without fear of being brought to justice. I knew that if either I or my family was targeted our fate would lie in our own hands. As a young boy I determined I would be strong enough to defend my loved ones. With that in mind I wanted to learn all I could about self-protection and how to turn ordinary implements into weapons. That was my motivation. My Christian background assured me that God lent his strength to righteous battle, so I prayed for help. I believed that the great angelic warrior Michael would assist me and that all of nature would be my *sensei*. With that belief, I became keenly observant and open to intuitive input. I built a *makiwara* (punching) post in my backyard in the shape of a man and began to work out daily. I sought books on martial theory and searched for any knowledgeable men willing to share insight with me. It was in an obscure book from Japan that I first learned about Bushido. This inner approach to martial ability appealed to me, and I began to cultivate the attitude of a samurai.

Under the guidance of Bushido, my posture became one which exuded power. My attitude declared that my fate was not in the hands of others but only within my own hands. Through the practice of Bushido my sense of powerlessness began to evaporate and my enthusiasm and techniques improved. Before long, people began to comment on the way I walked and sat. My countenance was becoming more warlike day by day. One day a bully who had always been able to defeat me with ease attacked me and without hesitation I blocked his assault and sent him to the ground with a single well-aimed blow to the solar plexus. He lay on the ground holding himself. His power over me was broken. I felt free. Now more than ever I carried myself with the warrior countenance. I was a beacon, warning would-be bullies to stay away from me.

Years later, after having moved from Virginia to New York and becoming a legendary defender of the weak because I did not hesitate to come to the rescue of victims of gangs or other practitioners of violence, I was plagued by a war within my mind. Family problems triggered emotional conflict that gave me no peace. Then one day after praying for guidance or relief, I was lead by the spirit within me to travel twenty-five miles to Greenwich Village. I met a man, dressed in a kimono, sitting with folded hands on a bench in Washington Square Park. The air around him was charged with peace. I was in bliss in his presence. Zen Master Nomura-Roshi, as he identified himself, invited me to come to his Zendo the next day. I bowed my agreement.

The very next day Roshi taught me the most simple yet profound technique of all. He taught me to sit . . . *shikantaza*.

All the written and spoken teachings about life, our true nature, and the arts are simply words until we actually experience the truth directly, become one with it, instead of standing apart from it as an observer. For there to be an observer there must be at least two. Oneness is not two. When the student of life and the arts practices *shikantaza*, a form of *zazen* (sitting), he lets go of himself and all concepts. Only when we let go of our intellectual grasping can reality reveal itself in its unvarnished simplicity. Only then can we function as we were intended to and not simply react.

After being initiated into the way of zazen by the Master, I continued to practice martial arts and do *shikantaza* as if there were no relationship between the two. Imagine how surprised I was when one day as I sat in meditation there was a melting away of barriers, a blaze of light, and I immediately understood the secret of self-defense from the inside out. There was no mystery. When I arose from my seat, I felt as if everything was clear to me. In keeping with Asiatic tradition, I spent the next few months seeking out Masters of the martial arts—Masters Moses

Power, Cleophus Jacobs, R. Yoshiteru Otani, Aaron Banks, and others—respectfully asking them to put my insight *(satori)* to the test. I was able to pass through whatever challenge was presented me. When I returned to Virginia, Master C.O. Neal of Juijitsu fame arranged a *menkyo* (trial by combat) and awarded me black belt ranking in *Wa-jitsu* (The Way of Accord) and *Aikijutsu* through the martial arts organization BUDO, a council sanctioned by the Highest Ranking Sensei and Masters in Hampton Roads, including Soke Kuniba, 9th-degree black belt and family head of Seishin Kai Shito-Ryu Karate. For years I became a favored demonstrator of the Zen and Aiki aspects of the martial arts.

My rise to prominence within the formal martial arts community created some jealousy among martial arts *sensei* who did not understand the Zen connection to the martial arts. Some wanted to challenge me to matches. I accepted as many of these challenges as I could, hoping to demonstrate the legitimacy of Zen practice in the martial arts. I felt that martial artists in the West were denying an essential aspect of the training. I demonstrated on television and accepted challenges on stage in a demonstration sponsored by the local newspaper. I took on all comers and continued this gruelling exercise until I felt my point had been proven. After that I limited demonstrations to police-sponsored events and to teaching in the *dojo* of Master Neal.

The point of my demonstrations was that my art was artless. It was no longer self-conscious. It arose effortlessly out of emptiness, out of no-knowledge. It was natural. The Zen definition of *natural* is "that which grows out of nothing." I had no art to brag about because there was no place within me to trace its origin. Movements came. My opponent was blocked, struck, or thrown through the air but without the sense of my exerting the action. There was action, but the action and the actor were a seamless thread. It was an incredible experience, like being blown about by the wind. I wanted my fellow warriors to experience the art to this depth, but how could I convey to them in words that the techniques I performed in fact were performing me? So-called normal men have a dualistic mind that works against itself. When that division is gone there is no observer within to critique or block action. When there is an impetus to act from outside of one's being . . . whoosh, the response comes from the holistic self.

My martial arts friends wanted me to share my techniques with them. I wanted to guide them beyond technique to the very source of martial creation. Their minds had been trained to see form and technique as the means to an end; they found it hard to conceive of a place that does not rely on form or technique. Body is form, the approach to defense is technique; but when these elements come together in the unconscious, there is no one applying technique. There is also no fear and no hesitation. The student is naturally humble because he cannot brag about movements which emerge without his conscious effort. It is the Inner Master who brings the enemy to his knees.

My experience proved to me that there is something within man which is greater than man himself. It is said that without acknowledgement of the Inner Master the outer Master will do the student no good. Our true teacher is always with us; the visible counterpart is to confirm and give form to what is already known deep within. In the West we have become so dependent on what we see that we have neglected the primary teacher. The Warrior Mind is focused within. It must draw mastery from itself. It cannot afford to look to the left or to the right in a struggle of life or death. Mind permeates all you see. If you give half of it to the opponent, you will be fighting yourself. Claim the sun, moon, and stars as your own; leave not a shred of mind to the enemy, and you will own the moment.

EMBRACE THE UNIVERSE

Your body is composed of the elements of nature—earth, wind, fire, and water—the ancients said. Your mind and spirit are beyond calculating. You are part of all you see and more. Embrace the universe as part of you. Receive the sun, the moon, the caverns, and the creatures who creep, crawl, and fly as part of your body and mind, and you will come to understand the uniqueness of man. You will experience harmony as you have never understood or felt it before. If you experience harmony, if you know it within yourself, you will easily sense any threat to that harmony. By their very nature, peace, love, and harmony are gifts which must be shared to be enjoyed. The stronger you grow in your love for peace and harmony, the greater will be your power to defend it. You will come to see that it is your duty as man to preserve the peace of the living universe, and that the living universe is none other than you.

There is order and symmetry in the universe. As

you meditate on this knowledge, you will come to see how you can keep this order. The tone of your voice and the movements of your body are all part of the dance of life. A word can disturb the peace, a smile can restore. The warrior will not use a sword when a flower can disarm the opponent more effectively. The highest warrior is one who seeks to preserve life, not to take it. When a warrior must physically move to protect himself, he must do so as a dance, performed without fear or anxiety. This dance is possible when we make the Warrior Mind part of our daily life, nothing special.

To become more aware of the dance of life, acknowledge the mystery of motion. Before you wash the dishes or scrub the floor, before you drive your car, bow in respect to the giver of life and mobility then meditate on your bodily activity as you go about the tasks. Just observe without comment or thought. Let the movement be your meditation. Being mindful of simple movement will give you a greater appreciation for the gift. In time, it will bring you greater mobility. You will come to respond fluidly to situations as they arise.

Although we are accustomed to taking things for granted, even ourselves, the warrior is a student of life. There is nothing that can be taken for granted. Mastery of an art, including the martial arts, comes from letting the art express itself through a willing (empty) vessel. Mastery comes not from asserting oneself but by negating the false self. Man *is* . . . but through no act of his own. If he is to realize his potential he must get out of his own way. Without self-consciousness, the world of nature—the universe—fulfills its destiny. The enlightened warrior is at home here. In times of peace he enjoys the peace. When the clouds of battle gather, his sword and arrows (or modern weapons) become his lightning and thunder. When the sun peeks through, the weapons are set aside.

The Warrior Mind is that mind which is always agile and alert, ready to adapt to any circumstance. It is a mind like water, rather than ice. It accommodates to the situation but has no fixed form. It is this mind that will be your friend no matter what is happening around you. The samurai learned to make his mind his best friend. Accomplishing this takes work. Our minds have been trained to serve others more so than ourselves. If there were no you there would be no others. First you must become enlightened before you can share that light with others. The warriors of old knew that we are defeated because the strong enemy knows how to find our *suki*, the weakness within the spirit of our mind. If you are weak you will not be very good for others or yourself. It is wise to study and grow strong, then your successes will touch more than you. They will be an inspiration to many. We are blessed by the offering of nature and the universe, but it is highly unlikely that they consciously praise themselves for serving us. If you be your best you have already contributed to others. Do not do good deeds self-consciously; this is vanity. There is no light in vanity, no Zen in clinging.

How is it that you see, hear, feel, taste, smell, and touch? Who is it that experiences these phenomena?

Do not seek an answer with your intellect. Just let the questions sink in. It is the experiencer of these things who acts to feed and clothe the body and moves to protect it from harm. Truly there is a marvelous being within us capable of great feats. Why do we shackle him from head to foot with our petty egos? It orders the sun to rise and orchestrates the planets in the universe, yet we doubt its power in us. Clinch your fist and strike empty space. Feel the rushing air as your hand sends the cosmos reeling. How can you doubt your true essence? See it reflected back in the eyes of all the men, women, and children you meet.

MO CHI CHU:
STRAIGHT AHEAD

No matter what you may think, life is straight ahead. We cannot turn back. Yet, although we know we cannot turn back in actuality, too many people turn their thoughts back to past days and lament the past. This is wasted energy. It is energy that is not available to us to meet the needs of today. The warrior faces the events which spring up in the present. He must dispatch with them and then move on. If we are to meet the events of the day with presence of mind we must stay focused on the arising moment. It is akin to driving a car and watching the road. If we are observant we can avoid even the unexpected car veering in our path. If we are not observing the road we may crash.

The road is not moving; the car is in motion. The Warrior Mind is immovable . . . it is life that is in motion. The tranquil mind can adapt to the changes as necessary. The warrior is selfless. That is, he harbors no fixed view of who or what he is. He leaves such thoughts to outsiders. Since he is not attached to a fixed identity, he is not bound to rigid behavior. He freely accommodates his action to the need. Too often we bind ourselves in a prison of words. We make ourselves obligated to our views to such a degree that we cannot move from them even if our well-being depends on such a move. The enlightened ones know that life has no fixed form although it is expressed in many forms. The warrior's power erupts from his freedom to flow from form to form without hesitation. By convention, a man may believe he is held together by his thoughts about himself. In reality, he is limited by this habit.

It is taught that when a warrior leaves his home for battle, he will never return if he looks back. It is best that he fixes his mind on the coming battle. The path home is through the battlefield. If you face a crisis, focus through it to the other side. Do not turn your face from it. By using this tact you teach your mind to solve the problem so that you may return to the desired path. The way to train the mind to deal with problems and dilemmas is to eliminate the possibility of escape. That is, you must realize that there is no alternative to facing the problem. When you determine that you must go straight ahead, straight through the problem, you develop the strength and courage needed to do so. Mind and spirit become directed to the task at hand. When your whole being is pointed straight ahead, a greater power than your own comes into play. This is the Tao (the Way) of old, that unexplainable wisdom to act, also known as the help of God.

Going straight ahead in spite of fear is an act of

faith. Faith alone reveals the transcendental power of Self. It opens avenues not apparent at other times. By pushing yourself to the limit you learn the secret of man. This knowledge is superior to the knowledge of who you are as an individual. The universal man lies beneath the limited role we play as egocentric beings. As you explore the potential which lies beneath the surface of your being, you discover that what we don't know about ourselves is far more fascinating than what we do know. Our unconscious abilities support what we know in marvelous ways.

The superior warrior charges straight ahead not because he is confident in what he knows but because he is certain that he can rely on the guidance of the Unknowable (God) to bring him through. The Warrior Mind clings to nothing. The essence of the Original Mind is nothing. As hard as this concept may be to grasp with the intellect, just this reliance on no thing is the foundation of superior art, be it the subtle moves of the warrior or the melodic gift of the musician.

Using our warrior metaphor again, if you were suddenly attacked without warning, you must let nature take its course. Do not stop your mind by harboring fear about your response. Go freely with your inspiration, one move after another, until the threat is behind you. This is *Mo Chi Chu*. When we act from our original nature, the act can be said to be spiritual. It is not self-conscious. From the spiritual act we come to appreciate the fundamental nature of life, that which lies beyond the ability of words to adequately capture.

The shimmering sun . . .
The whispering wind . . .
A bird flying in the sky above . . .
is undisturbed by his reflection
in the water below.

The Great Sensei fills the universe. He teaches us through all things, but He communicates directly into the spirit of man; He does not teach the mind. The mind seeks to approximate the truth in words, but words are limited in their power to convey. The Great Sensei would have us become doers and conveyers of truth by our actions and bearing, not pundits who talk a good game.

Peace is superior to war. You cannot defend the peace if you have no peace to defend. Become peace. Become love. Do these two things well and the Warrior Mind is established in you.

THE ONE

There is no head higher than your own. There is no head lower than your own. You are the human being. All other human beings are reflections of you, as you are of them. You must respect yourself for the honor that has been given you to walk in the likeness of the Creator himself. Whether you are a doctor or a janitor makes no difference, for you are the likeness of the Creator as doctor or the likeness of the Creator as janitor. You may know the secret of life just as well from either role. The taste of tea is just as hot and wet for you as for any world leader. Nature does not slight you for your lack of social standing. You are the One for it is only you who feels, thinks, and acts out life in this space. You are worthy. Let your actions demonstrate the dynamic power of this life which has formed itself as you.

When you sit, walk, or move, do so with author-ity. It is through the medium of our bodies that we come to know the Master one-on-one in the middle ground between stillness and motion, between silence and thought. When we look upon ourselves as the expression of the Creator our ordinary activity becomes acts of worship and appreciation. Every event becomes part of the drama of life.

We coexist with our Creator, the Great Sensei, and we miss the point of our daily struggles if we do not acknowledge this coexistence. But if we claim the realm of consciousness as our own, we would be wise to accept the realm of the unconscious, that of spiritual input, as belonging to the Inner Master, Himself. Although we can speculate about the conscious and how we should speak or act, we cannot begin to comprehend the movements of the Master. We can shadow Him, however, by the process of self-surrender, of letting go of our preconceived plan or strategy to cast our fate totally upon Him. This is impossible to do unless your faith is such as to accept that there is indeed a ground of being, an intelligence which lies behind your own to take over when you let go. This is the Zen level of activity. It is also the way of any person who has cast his or her fate to God above logic or self. When one has truly let go, a new life emerges . . . the Way manifests. You become the One.

There is only One after all. If there is man, He must be you. You are the one consciously breathing and experiencing life at this moment. You can only speculate about me. If *you* don't count, who does? How can anyone else fulfill man's destiny for you? If you don't come to experience the truth of your nature it won't matter if everyone else in the world does. The knowledge that everyone else in the world has a full belly will not satisfy your hunger. You must eat for yourself. So if you desire to improve the world, save it, then turn to the mirror and save yourself. When you know the taste of salvation thoroughly, your light will cast the darkness out of 10,000 lives.

The evil one strikes at you as he does countless victims, but you repel him with all your might. You bring him to his knees, causing him to doubt his power. By coming to the aid of your self you have weakened the enemy of men in general; you have championed the Good. The Good is not weak, but it needs a vessel to contain its power. Be that vessel. Desire what is good for yourself. Who can trust a man who does not want what is good for himself but claims to care about the rest of us?

You are the One. If you love life and the good things of life, you will work to preserve them, not fight against them. Become a vessel of the Good. Let the light that is in man shine through you so that we all may see your strength and grace and celebrate the virtuosity of our Creator. There is no vanity in this. All things come from the One. The secret of the One is hidden in us. It is revealed when we follow the traceless way of the Spirit. Our arts link us to our original home. The warrior learns to dance with death. His is a living art. He becomes one with the great enemy by finding a rhythm which affirms life even when there are those who try to take it away. Such a warrior never loses his focus on life even in the midst of the most horrendous battle. The One is life; there is no place in the One for death.

At all times the Warrior Mind is moving from one life-affirming act to another. Life is your goal. Life is your only focus. Zen people say that there are two kinds of swords—the sword that kills and the sword that saves. You wield the sword that saves. You clench your fist to preserve life and well-being, not to take it away.

FLOWING WITH THE WIND

When I am in the right state of mind, my art is simply to flow with the wind. My body moves as if it is carried aloft by a breeze. It adapts to the movement of my opponent effortlessly. The art reveals itself to me through my relaxed state. I find that the experience is akin to writing poetry. My poetic response to life comes of its own as I loosely hold my pen. Can I be said to be writing poetry or receiving poems from their source? The process of creation for me is a cooperation between my conscious mind and its unconscious counterpart. There is a partnership like that illustrated in the black-white yin yang symbol. I experience myself as yin, the passive receiver of the active power, yang. I suspect that the average person sees himself or herself as the active or yang force, that which is the initiator of action.

The wind cannot be seen, but Zen lore reminds us that a tree gives bodily form to the wind. Our body, like the tree, is the visible manifestation of that which cannot be seen. It can show us what is negative or that which is positive. It can also demonstrate that which lies beyond the duality of negative and positive, good and evil. The Bible tells us that it is just that place beyond the division of good and evil that God chose for man to dwell. Anything less than a return to our primordial roots can be nothing more than second best. What the Creator intended was that man should draw from a place within himself that was not dependent on knowing, as God does, himself. The original man was capable of flawless action without even the possibility of second thought. This is freedom as only the enlightened can know. Ordinary man is haunted by fear of failure, paralyzed by the thought that he might make a mistake.

The art of the warrior is good for teaching us to move beyond such fears. In a real-life battle, hesitation could mean instant death. Responding with accuracy and speed could mean life. There is no recourse but to learn to give oneself to the action . . . to merge with the wind and let the outcome be what it may. We must learn to trust the wind.

A pilot must believe that the wind will hold up his plane. Skydivers learn to rest upon the invisible blanket of air as they glide through their maneuvers. The wind is a euphemism for your true . . . the Original Mind. You can learn its power only by releasing yourself to it.

There are many ways to flow with the wind. One way is to trust yourself to be yourself. "When you are you Zen is Zen," Suzuki Roshi said. Playing a fixed role day after day as if following a script is going against the wind. You must learn to release the pressure on yourself to conform in so many ways so that the true you emerges. What really is your favorite music? What are your true views on politics? When we hold back the truth of ourselves in even these ways we dam the flow of the power within us. There is only one of you. You are a star in your own right. However, your light will not shine if you emulate everything and everyone. To freely express the real you, you cannot hold to a false image at the same time. One must either let go or hold on. The true you emerges when there is no attempt to prove anything to anyone. There is no difference between responding to a question and responding to a blow. In each case the mind is engaged. The warrior's path is natural; that is, it promotes effortless response. Can a man or woman who has no fear of death be afraid to live or assert his or her true identity before all comers?

Christians are taught, "As the wind which bloweth where it listeth, and thou heareth the sound thereof but knoweth not from whence it cometh or wither it goeth, so are they that are born of the spirit." Truly the Way is not to be found in the realm of cognitive knowledge. The Zen approach to the arts and life begins precisely at the point of this scripture. It is a practice which has as its sole aim pointing to that experience which is beyond our verbal ability. It is a reminder that outside of our vain conceptions is a living experience which is infinitely more vital. Words may miss the point but we can demonstrate its truth in endless refreshing ways.

When I stand on the mat rooted in the grace of this awesome experience and see my opponents fly through the air and fall at my feet without conscious effort on my part, when I feel my body rise and fall with the cosmic breath, I am humbled by life. I realize that somehow, mysteriously, I am a partaker of something greater than I can comprehend . . . I am embraced by this greatness which is breath of my breath. I bow in humility. My only desire is to empty myself more, to pour out the false thoughts I had been taught which set me up in contrast to the world which is in fact nothing less than my own body. I help my *uke* (opponent) to his feet, grateful that through his attack I have learned something more about the true nature of being. Learning is not really the proper word. It is really *unlearning* that I am doing. The wind does not know how it blows or builds in power but it moves in impressive ways nonetheless.

ABANDON TECHNIQUE

If I tossed you a ball and your right hand moved
to catch it, could you catch it with a closed fist? In
order to catch with a hand you must abandon the fist
to release the open palm. In the same manner, if we
want to meet life with our full mental resources we
must stop using the mind to hold on to our conception of life. After all is said and done, we are merely
holding on to a fixed image, not reality at all. Reality
is in a constant state of change. Like the old saying,
you cannot put your foot in the same stream twice . . .
the water has moved and is still moving. When you
release yourself from the impossible dilemma of holding onto something that is not tangible, your mind is
free to work in the realm of its own mastery . . . the
seen. The place of the mind is simply to function in
the realm of the seen. By our humility we acknowledge the Master . . . the Spirit, Lord of the unseen
and the unknowable.

What are we talking about from the practical

standpoint of a warrior? If a man is threatening you, you can see and hear him, but you do not know for certain what he will do. Watch him with a calm mind, stay focused and relaxed. Do not attempt to guess what the opponent will do. Instead, trust in your spirit. Only your spirit has the ability to act without necessity of thought in perfect union with what actually happens. The mind's duty is to be still, to surrender to the spirit. This is the hardest act for those trained in the European approach to mind. For while most men give lip service to existence of God or Spirit on Sunday, they do not defer to Him on Monday. "He who is within you is greater than he who is in the world," says the scripture. This verse means that the Spirit within is greater than anything in the world, even mind. Mind functions in the world, Spirit emanates from that point before the world was even formed.

The warrior knows from practical experience that the Inner Power is greater than his conscious skill. For that reason the most revered among the ancient warriors was the gentle Master who seemingly had no formal skills. It was said that "the true Master carries no sword." This could also mean that the real Master relies on no conscious skill. He does not depend on what can be seen. An old story illustrates this point.

A young archer gloried in his skill. He could outshoot everyone in his province. He sought to test his skill against those in other villages. At some point in his journey, he was told of an old man who was said to be the greatest archer of the region. The young man, full of himself, sought out the old man to challenge him. He found the old man sitting in a hut in the mountains.

When he heard why the young man had come, the old archer was not inclined to give him a contest. He had nothing to prove. The young man was insistent, however, so the aged one finally agreed to demonstrate his skill. He took the young man to a place high on the mountain, where the two of them stood on a precipice. There was a log connecting one side of the mountain path to the other. Below was the ground.

"Stand on the log and shoot at the geese above," the old man directed. The young archer trembled at the thought of risking his life on the log. Yet, he did not want to fail so he summoned his will and ventured out. Balancing himself precariously, he sought a target in the sky and steadied his arm. Notching an arrow, he fired. Three birds were pierced through by a single shot. He came back to safety, smug in his belief that the old man could not beat his performance.

"You call that archery," the old man teased. Then, with no bow or arrow visible, he leapt out onto the log and stretched forth his naked arm. Concentrating on his imaginary bow, he released a shot. A bird plummeted from the air. The mouth of the young man fell open in shock.

"How can you practice archery without a bow?" he asked.

"How can you call yourself an archer when you still need a bow?" He responded.

In this way the young man learned that the way of mastery is beyond form and technique. It is beyond comprehension.

In the West we are accustomed to separating Church from State and in that spirit our spiritual understanding from our secular life. In the Zen-yogi approach to life, the spiritual and secular are recognized as one. Making shoes can be a spiritual act if the person who is making the shoes does so with a spiritual mind. *Spiritual* does not mean the dogmatic approach of religion which focuses on conscious beliefs. *Spiritual* means to function by the leading of the spiritual rather than by the conscious dictates of the mind. The spiritual mind embraces the feminine way; it yields. The ego-mind is aggressive as it acts from the state of knowing, calculating and analyzing; it stops and goes. The spiritual mind does not stop. It is *mo chi chu*. It goes straight ahead. It is direct. All things are possible to the spiritual mind.

The Zen Master often refers to the Original Mind as a mirror. If we use this analogy, the ego-mind is that which is turned toward substances. It may reflect a tree or a flower. The spiritual mind is turned toward No-thing. What is the image of a mind turned toward No-thing? Such a mind instantly reflects what is presented before it, but it does not change its true nature. It has no true form of its own.

Its nature cannot be apprehended by form. This is in keeping with the Biblical saying that man is made in the image of God. "The word man comes from the Sanskrit word for mental being . . . *manu*," says Satguru Sant Keshavadas. Since God cannot be grasped by form, the word "likeness" cannot be referring to our arms, legs, torso and head. Obviously, it is our inner nature which is in the likeness of God . . . marvelous awareness, creative and responsive . . . mysterious.

The fall of man is revealed to be his quest for "other" or outside knowledge. Man is still falling because he still values outside teachings over the revelations of his own Inner Master. Not so the warrior. The warrior knows that the Inner is the all and all of his life and the "other" is illusory at best. He trusts his life to the Inner Master because his life originates from the Inner Master. It is the trick of the enemies of man to pull him outside of himself, outside of the oneness, so that he may be vulnerable to defeat.

THE BOXER

When I was new in the study of Bushido, I learned a valuable lesson in a fight with a neighborhood bully. A friend came to my house to tell me my brother was being beaten up. I ran after him to the scene of the trouble. When I arrived I pushed my brother to safety and stood in his place; confident that I would prevail, I took a Jujitsu stance.

"Oh no. You can't use that stuff," the bully said. "It's not fair. You have to box."

Listening to him, I switched my stance to the imitation of a boxer's. I felt uncomfortable and unsure of myself. In seconds fists were flying in the air and we were jostling for position. We both fell to the ground, holding on to each other. In the wild flailing of fists, he caught me in my eye, then declared the fight over although I had not surrendered. Even though he connected with my eye by accident, the rumor mill exaggerated the results and the youth was hailed as the big victor. He had stopped the fight before I could retaliate, but I had allowed it.

I learned from that incident to never let the opponent dictate strategy. When I departed from my way of fighting and adopted the method that was his stronghold I ensured his victory. The fact that he did not want me to approach the fight with Jujitsu proved he felt a psychological disadvantage. I let him shift the disadvantage to me.

The Jujitsu Way was how I expressed my growing warrior nature at the time. It was the way my defensive mechanism naturally manifested. I had to consciously try to box. As long as my mind was engaged in trying to figure out how to box I was not able to fight from the state of *mushin* (No Mind) which is the manner of Bushido.

The defender is under no obligation to adapt his style to please his attacker. The defender must be free to respond as appropriate to preserve his own life and well-being. To become conscious of what the enemy wants you to do is to be self-conscious, to run the risk of being paralyzed with indecision. Bodily we should take a strong, confidence stance. Mentally we should remain feminine, yielding, empty of a preconceived course of action.

The Way works when there is no hesitation between action and reaction. This means that the body is responsive to the inner nature. It bobs and weaves, ducks and dips in accord with the movement of the opponent with no division between the act of the attacker and your response. Such mirror-like response comes only when body, mind, and spirit are in proper relationship. Although we speak of them in this trilateral way, they are One . . . you.

The world outside seeks to tear us from our True Place. It largely succeeds. Only you can find the way back. It is a journey you must take alone. A teacher can give you guidance and outline the principles and pitfalls of the journey, but the gate allows only one to enter. The gate is within you. You know how far you have gotten by the way you respond to the myriad stimuli of the world. Are you confident and serene in the daily battles or are you disturbed and stressed-out? The world may not change but a person has the power to be transformed, to "stand above, pass on, and be free." One person can rise beyond the mud of existence like a lotus blossom, be beautiful like the Rose of Sharon in the midst of ugliness.

In any activity, there is the presence of form and movement. To the uninitiated eye this constitutes technique. The conscious mind is aware of the technique to be used. This is not *mushin*.

This is not spiritual activity. The Warrior Mind as it functions from the spiritual state moves the body from one form to the next without the need of words or images. There is just action arising out of "emptiness" . . . the unknown. The experience of such action is life-affirming and breathtaking. It is an expression of oneness. There is no second thought.

If we are to experience the oneness which comes from acting from the traceless depths of the spiritual mind we must practice letting go of second thoughts. The second thought is a result of our mistrust of our own natural mind. We were taught to doubt our

fundamental nature by men and women who either
did not trust their own minds or consciously set out
to weaken our faith in our own power as men and
women. With diminished faith in ourselves we are
easily manipulated by outside forces. The prescrip-
tion for this ailment comes from Zen Master Bankei.
He said that we should act as though there is no possibility of interference by second thoughts. We must
deny the validity of second thoughts. If I offer you
two items and said choose one right away, you may
freeze with hesitation. You must learn to pick one
right away and not fool yourself into believing that
slow deliberation is always best. The conscious mind
is doubtful. It was made so by those who berated our
decisions in the past. The Unconscious or spiritual
mind knows precisely what to do without knowing
how. The word *knowledge* includes the word *know*.
Wisdom contains the word *is*. It just is.

Suzuki-Roshi tells us to relax and let Buddha
take care of the track (the path). By that he means
that when we relax into Original Mind it knows
where to go and what to do on its own. We can trust
Original Mind to do what is best for us. To justify
that faith we must raise the Original Mind from its
abyss through practice. Practice does not create the
Original Mind. It is always there, perfect, brilliant,
even if we never experience it. Practice simply
demonstrates its power.

Only when we have allowed the Original Mind
to surface do we know the wonderful nature given to
man and can appreciate the awesome gift of human
life to its fullest. At this moment we can act without

doing because we coexist with the Creator. "I would that they be One as we are One," Jesus Christ prayed. If you as man insist upon functioning from yang, the masculine force, you will never know oneness. God as Creator is yang; the student must by definition take the position of yin, the feminine energy. He must become the valley which by lying low receives the refreshing waters which cascade down the mountainside. As observed by the Masters through the ages, when yin receives yang the combination results in a third power which is the manifestation of the Way. What Siddhartha Gotama demonstrated in nature as the Buddha was shown in its supernatural manifestation by Jesus the Christ. Siddhartha demonstrated the Original Mind as it functioned in the everyday world. Christ represented man's spiritual roots. The two paths are not the same but the spiritual path of Christ outlined the need for mental discipline—One Mind training—as well. This is largely overlooked by the Christian church, explaining why so many ministers are suspicious of meditation, as if meditation were evil. Yet without meditation, which is mentioned in the Bible often, there can be no One Mind. The carnal mind—that is, the mind that is identified with the body—constantly wars with the spirit, even in the most faithful of believers. The training of the mind is a science which produces proven results. It is not a dogma to believe but a series of techniques to be applied to re-orient or renew the mind.

My mother plays the piano. On the days she plays particularly well she says, "God anointed my fingers. The Holy Spirit made me play better."

Those who really have a personal experience with God know that her experience is not unique. In fact, the word *yoga* means "union with God." It is based on the disciple offering himself and his activity to the direction of God so that he might submerge his ego in the grace of God. The yogi wants to be a complete instrument of God. Using that definition, any faithful believer in God who offers his mind, body, and spirit back to the Creator of all things would by definition be a yogi. His yoga could be music, shoe-shining, martial arts, or any discipline, art, or work through which God could demonstrate his power.

We must not forget that words are only tools of communication. They stand for something else. People who speak different languages may be speaking about the same thing in different ways. The spiritual warrior uses the appropriate tool no matter what it is called. Words are arbitrary, it is the spirit behind the message that is all-important. When we step back and let the Spirit of God flow through us, all of our arts, disciplines, and works are raised to a higher level. We are fully aware that something more than "we" is at work. When others see the grace with which we perform, it is our duty to give the praise back to God. Thus the yogi diverts praise from himself by saying, "*Neti neti* [Not me, not me]," and the Asian martial arts master bows and says, "It is nothing." They mean it. When we are in the feminine state of mind we are played as an instrument, and it feels wonderful. It is said, "In Buddhism there is no room for effort." The Original Mind, in other words, acts without effort.

This points us right back to the mind of Adam in the Garden of Eden. While some men pursue greater worldly knowledge, there are those who have quietly abandoned the technique of arrogant men and humbly sought to return to the mind that the Creator set up for man. He left a clue, as we have mentioned: "to return, come with the mind of a child." Abandon the love of technique; it is all right to practice techniques but let them go when the session is over. Use technique as the toy of a child; pick it up, let it drop. Face your task, be it an opponent or a job, with a mind empty of anxiety or thought. Let the miracle of activity come.

THE WAY OF FORM
AND
NOTHINGNESS

As a student of Satguru Sant Keshavadas, I learned that the body is not the self. In the Western world we commonly think that it is. The Chinese Zen Master Sheng-Yen wrote of the body in his *Chlan* [Zen] *Newsletter*. Describing his approach to the *shikantaza* (silent illumination) method of meditation, he said:

> . . . *be aware of your body, but do not think of it as yourself. Regard your body as a car you drive. You have to handle the car well, but it is not you. If you think of your body as yourself, you will be bothered by pain, itchiness and other vexations. Just take care of the body and be aware of it.* . . . *You have to be mindful of your body as the driver must be mindful of the car, but the car is not the driver.*

The classical warrior was aware of this principle. The unarmed fighter made his body into a weapon. Master Moses Power of Vee Jujitsu fame once said that "man is the superior weapon." If you think of your body as a vehicle which you propel by the power of your will you will understand how a clenched fist or an open hand can be used as a weapon. They are missiles, no less than a rock or a stick. It is all in how you view your body. If you think of it as *you*, you may be overprotective and hesitant. If you think of it as *an instrument*, as you do a weapon held in your hand, you will have the type of detachment you need to excel in action. Superior action takes place only when the mind is in a state of nonattachment. Clinging to your body protectively can get you hurt or killed more quickly than you know, although it may seem as though the opposite is true. The mind that is not attached to things, including the body, is free to act as it wills without thought or reflection. This is the action prized by Masters; it is like a flash of lightning.

The spiritual teachers have always emphasized spirit over the body, but the old attachment to flesh is hard to break. Spirit is not discernible by the senses or comprehendible by the intellect, but by nonattachment to mind and body it reveals itself through activity. That is why work, the arts, and various disciplines are excellent ways to experience our spirituality. Spirit must be taken on faith; faith demonstrates itself in works (activity). "Faith without works is dead," the Bible reveals. The Inner Way of expressing spirituality is through some activity, even serving a cup of tea or sweeping a floor in the spirit of the Master. Too often in the West we choose to discuss or argue points of religion. To go from carnal mind to spiritual mind, the mind must mirror the spirit. The virtues of the spirit are serenity, love, spontaneity, creativity, and straightforwardness, among other things. The spiritual mind is focused in the present. It is said that God is Omni-All Present. To be in the likeness of something means that one is similar. Since man (mind or mental being) is said to be in the likeness of God, he must have similar attributes, scaled down though they might be.

The exercises we practice were designed to free us from the errors we make with the mind. We abuse the mind and are abused by it because we have failed to take seriously the teachings on the mind left by spiritual teachers down through the ages. This is a sad commentary on the vanity of men. The only way possible to work on the mind is to do so from a vantage point beyond the mind. That leaves only the spiritual level. One can work on the body with the mind, but we need to withdraw to the refuge of the spirit in order to train the mind. If this is not done we are left to the impossible task of trying to achieve oneness of mind by further dividing it into teacher and pupil. We can never succeed in this way. That is why Shunryu Suzuki-Roshi said it is absolutely necessary to believe in nothing—that is, something beyond intellect and the senses (God). Only from the resting place afforded by relaxing into this nothingness, as in the person of the Holy Spirit, can we find healing for the mind. He also made the point that, although men think they created cars and air-planes and other inventions, they were wrong: "Since God created man, he also created cars and airplanes, etc." The word *nothing* is a device. It is to keep the meditator from developing concepts or images in lieu of having the living experience of the Truth. Make no mistake, the Truth, the Way, is a living, ongoing experience for which no words will ever suffice to adequately describe. In our country we are accustomed to thinking we know something because we have words for it. That will not work here. It is simply a case of show, not tell. "Let your light so shine before men that they may see your good works and glorify the Father which is in heaven." Your body is in the world of the seen. It is the means by which you demonstrate your understanding for other men to see. The tongue may impress the uninitiated but not those who have tasted the steaming tea of spiritual insight for themselves.

Even the most spiritual of warriors uses his body. He needs to take care of it as he would a good horse or his automobile. If it is healthy and supple, it will serve the spiritual mind better. It will be a testament to his growth in understanding.

The basic equipment of all men is the same although it may function at different levels. You must not compare yourself to anyone else. Your path is to express only what you are, to discover that which is laid out for you to do and to be. If you discover that path you are successful before the Council of the Universe and your Creator. Remember: when you are *you*—*that* is enlightenment.

As a warrior you will discover a natural way to move your own body, a way that feels right and comfortable to you. Explore these natural movements. Let yourself dance out the forms and feel where they want to go. Feel them, do not picture them. I call this *the art of dancing to no-music.* We will explore this theme further in the next chapter.

THE ART OF DANCING
TO NO-MUSIC

As I sat in my meditation room practicing *shikantaza* (just sitting, with an attitude of faith) I was suddenly wiped from existence. I know this only because my consciousness returned point by point until I was aware of the most minute particle of existence. I observed from some unknown place as that particle multiplied in a dance that created the universe, making use of sound and ever-expanding rhythm. In the final moments of the experience the rhythm caught me up as a breath. There was breath but no me to be seen. This rhythm became feeling and the feeling brought me back home to bodily existence. When I started to stand I found my body had stood without my sensing motion. Whatever move I willed took place as if I were spirit rather than flesh and blood. It was awesome and serene. I was in peace, a peace which mirrored my encounter with the Spirit of Christ when I was a boy. It filled my body the same way. The difference in the two events was that in the second I received information, a memory of my original place in the scheme of things before I was born. I saw man shorn of all his trappings and the universe in its naked reality. One of the most powerful revelations, however, was the place of rhythm in the life of man . . . the dance of life.

The warrior must be aware of rhythm. There is rhythm in a battle. There is always rhythm where there is more than one. The warrior must find the place of stillness within his body-mind and move in accord with the rhythm all around him. This is the dance of life.

The rider mounted on a horse is not the beautiful beast, but when they move in synchronization they are said to move as one. You are not the body, but like a horse you can ride it in synchronization and it will respond to your will, easily, and you will move as one. You are the spirit—that is, a formless reality. The link between you and the body is the bridle we call the mind. If the horse (body) controls the bridle, the rider may be in for a rough ride or find himself thrown to the ground. If the spirit controls the bridle, the body-horse will serve the rider well. It is said that a savage beast can be soothed by music. There is the music which comes from man who because of his divided mind hears the universal sound in only a fractured version and there is the music of the Spirit whose melody is healing and whole. The music of the Spirit heals the fractured mind and soothes the beast at the same time. By music I do not just mean the music we hear with our ear but the soundless melody we pick up only with our spiritual ear. It is that sweet music of the Creator the gurus call *shabd*.

The rhythm is life. As you learn to move your body in response to the inner rhythm it will always respond as it should in emergencies. It will act appropriately because it will be guided by the all-seeing spiritual essence within and not by the finite senses led by the ego. The mark of a spiritual Master is humility. He is aware that his skill emerges from a place that is above his ability to grasp, so he does not brag. All human beings possess the same level of being, but not all of us have access to the higher teachings. The events in the physical world are metaphor for our understanding on either the mental or spiritual levels. Your actions reveal your mastery or lack of it. Do not dance based on what your ego perceives or you will be misled. Instead, feel within for that soundless rhythm and let it guide you moment by moment, movement by movement, just as if you were dancing to the music of your favorite band.

LIGHTNING FLASHES,
THUNDER ROLLS

To understand the potential which lies within you for action on all levels, you have only to observe nature. When a brilliant lightning bolt cuts through the air, the sound of thunder follows. It needs no instruction to express itself, it simply does. When the sunlight shines on a flower, the flower turns its face to meet it and receives the light of its life. The flower does not "know" how to do this. In the same way, birds build nests and rabbits bore holes because it is their nature to do so. They are able to act appropriately without internal resistance. They act single-mindedly to perform the desired task.

Now although we as intelligent creatures look at nature as if we are beyond it, we are not. Our bodies and minds are part of everything we see. What we have done is mentally hold ourselves aloof from our environment as we have learned to conquer it. Doing so is like wrestling the left side of the body with the right. Through meditation, the healing exercise for the mind, we come to see that this view of nature is false. We are all swimming in the great ocean that is universe on one hand and God on the other. When we rely on the intellect as our sole instrument of learning, we see only partially. "We see through a glass darkly," said the Apostle Paul. Western civilization prides itself on the accomplishments of its intellect. We have built rich nations, teeming with material abundance for all to see. But by putting so much emphasis on the seen, the object of the senses, we have denied our higher faculties, the fruits or gifts of the Spirit. We are Spirit, too. Only Spirit can access Spirit.

If we raise our spirit on Sunday morning we will be spiritual on Sunday morning. If we raise our spirit on Monday, we will be spiritual on Monday. Religion is the ritual of worship and learning about God. Being spirit is a matter of fact and realization. You may believe you are spirit, but have you had direct perception and proof of your spiritual nature? Spiritual nature is a seven-days-a-week proposition just as having a body and mind covers each day. Our arts, all arts, give us tools to explore our spirit. Creativity comes from the spiritual level of our being. If we mentally approach our art with the proper attitude we will come to appreciate the source of our creativity and the source of our being in an intimate way. It is in this area that our Asian brothers and Native people in so-called uncivilized lands excel. They approach their work and art with the realization that they flow from a sacred stream, whether that source is called Buddha (meaning that power which is beyond grasping and verbalization), the Great Spirit, God, Jehovah, or Brahmin. All are pointing to the same experience in different languages. As they work with clay or wood, fashion a work of art from raw form, they mirror the Creator in the work of forming the universe. They make contact with His Spirit through their spirit and their lives are taken to a different level of being that others may not suspect.

The artists who do not approach their work in this way claim themselves as sole authors of their works. They believe ego-self is the creator of all good things not found in nature. They have this false perception because they have no idea what their self really is. This can only be ascertained by giving up false views and letting go of self. Meditation is a tool which unknots the fingers of the ego, so we can fall back into ultimate reality. This is not what preachers mean when they speak of knowing God and "salvation." There is a difference between accepting the Spirit of God as real and realizing the truth of who you are. Most people who profess to love God do so with their mind but have failed to receive him in the fullness of their spirit; as a result they are not yet free beings. Is not God the giver of paradise and freedom? He never took away our freedom; we did that all by ourselves. We must find the way back. The problem is in how we perceive ourselves. We are listening to the wrong masters.

God will certainly help us when we cry out spiritually, but the mental realm is our territory, our power field from which we fail or succeed. We must work to restore our mind to its natural glory and spontaneous way. To achieve that realization we must start with the simplest truth. We did not make ourselves, so why do we think we can do a good job of making ourselves over? In truth, despite the fancy gadgets man produces as a matter of course outside of spiritual input, man has ruined his nature. The most civilized people have proven they are capable of great inhumanity to man and can satisfy their souls with logical justifications and explanations. Man broke the Original Mind by causing it to violate its nature, and we continue to do that day after day. In the original man, intellect followed wisdom; that is, man simply understood whatever he desired to know and acted freely without forethought. He could reflect at his leisure, after the fact. After his infamous fall, he could no longer access the wisdom of the Creator at will but had to rely on logic to piece together knowledge in order to act. He went from acting effortlessly out of wisdom to having to stop and figure out solutions, knowing he could be wrong.

In a life-and-death battle, a warrior could not afford to hesitate. That is why the superior warrior learned to rely on what many called the Spirit of Heaven—guidance from an untraceable and unim-peachable source. When this power manifested with-in him, the warrior felt his arms and legs gain new power and the path his weapon would take was already decided before he had a thought. He knew he could trust this power to lead him through the bat-tle, so he learned to let go of himself and merge into the oceanic presence, to go with the Inner Master, wherever he wanted to lead. These warriors were the *meijin* (the geniuses) whose art no one could explain. Yet they were humble.

The humility comes from understanding that your ability arises out of the depth of your being and existed before you were born. It is the power of all men, but they do not suspect it. As long as you act from the limited perception of ego, of I and you, you will miss the truth. When mind lets go of its image of self and its accumulated beliefs about the self, only then can the true *meijin* appear in his unspoiled glory. When the *meijin* appears, Adam rejoices and paradise is regained. Unfortunately, only the *meijin* will experience this paradise, even though all human beings and animals are walking around in it. Each person must open the gate for himself. The arts are our tools to use in our everyday world so that we may constantly stay plugged into the Great Power.

In the West we carry ourselves with a kind of vanity even when we worship. In the East it is customary to bow. A bow is a way of actually offering your body and mind to the Creator, so that he may receive it and purify our thoughts and actions. It is a demonstrated attitude of recognition, a way of saying I acknowledge your presence in all I do. I see you in everyone. Personally, I bow, even here in America. It increases the power of my spirit over my mind and body; it causes me to feel the presence of the Master in the most mundane situations. It reminds me I am but His student . . . always.

To believe in yourself is simply to acknowledge that He who made you did a great job. He made you from perfection, but placed you in an imperfect shell. Now, what can you make of this challenge? Know that all you need is within you. Nothing comes from the outside but distraction and the Great Lie. You are the only man or woman in the world that can make a difference . . . you. If not you, who?

Because you were perfectly conceived, you know what to do. It is there. You just must prove it to yourself. Test the power. Test God. He likes that. You are placing your visible body in the care of an invisible Master, who loves you, as part and parcel of Himself. I know your question. What about the other guy? If he were to acknowledge the Inner Master in the same way as you, you would be evenly matched and there would be no loser or winner. This has been proven in battles over and over again, so there is nothing to worry about. The Inner Master will not defeat Himself. But where He is not acknowledged in your opponent, you are the clear victor . . . always. This has been my experience.

When I speak of the Inner Master I do not want people to think it is akin to possession or anything like that. The Inner Master works through the unconscious mind, the realm of no-thought. You are guided silently and wisely. Your confidence is flawless. The Inner Master is, in fact, none other than God, Himself, manifesting through you . . . so what else is new? Whatever we can do, God can do better. If you are a musician, He is a musician. If you are a writer, He is a writer. If you are a warrior, He is the ultimate warrior. Who can be a better teacher than the Creator of all things? Even in the modern age men have tapped into the infinite wisdom of God and His universe to draw forth wisdom in a given field. O Sensei Morihei Uyeshiba founded the art of Aikido based on a spiritual insight he gained in a fight. Uyeshiba was a Christian martial artist. He revealed that he learned that the true nature of the martial arts was to receive the Spirit of the Universe and to spread His peace. Thus Aikido, when practiced by those who respect the original revelation, is a beautiful and serene approach to the warrior arts. Prior to Uyeshiba's experience, he was faithfully pursuing the work of Christ in a uniquely Japanese church. His enlightenment experience was a by-product of his faith in God.

To be sure, inventions are made every day by people who don't acknowledge the reality of God. It is man's nature to create. But the people who fail to seek the spiritual level of life are missing out on a great treasure the likes of which they cannot imagine. The mind cannot get beyond mind, so it cannot work on itself. Only spirit is over mind and can discipline and guide it to greater heights. Man is in the likeness of his Creator, but he cannot access his powers properly without studying the Way of God, Himself. When we learn how wonderfully we are made we will want to correct our errors and let the real self emerge like a wonderful blossom from the earth. We cannot take heaven by storm. We must be obedient little children and sit still at our Father's feet. Then, by virtue of His Holy Spirit, He will teach us all things.

I do not tell you about God and the Inner

Master or even the Original mind so that you can believe what I say as a form of gospel. I share these thoughts with you for you to seek out and practice within yourself in search of the True Way of Action. All men are the same. Do not be deceived. We eat, drink, defecate, sleep, and procreate. We all have body, mind, and spirit. We are the same in every way that matters but have different experiences based on our environment and opportunity. Fundamentally, we are all alike. We owe our origin to the same phenomenon. The Truth is One. Men argue over words about the Creator, but it does not matter—Truth is still one. When you enter into the realm of stillness (meditation), faith, love, and action, the words cease to be a barrier. The Truth scatters darkness by its Light, and you are certain of the Path.

Truth transforms, love protects the object of that love, and faith manifests as action. You will know and your actions will speak to the mind and spirit of others. In the West there is too much talk and intellectual discussion about God. We need more meditation (listening) to balance out the prayer and talk, and more demonstrations of love. Religions give God a bad name. Enlightened actions, virtuosity of all kinds, testify to his handiwork.

The karma yogi is that disciple who seeks to know God through action. He offers all his actions to God, good and bad. By offering his speech, his work, his arts to God, the karma yogi invites God to teach him through all actions. This is what the spiritual warrior does. He denies his ego so as to allow God-Spirit to teach him through the movements of his body. This is different from consciously moving your own body. Rest assured, God will take you up on the offer and you may be shocked to find He can block a punch without your help or paint a more sensitive picture than you could on you own. When this happens to a student of the Way, he or she discovers what living is all about. This is Oneness. Nothing can compare to this experience. It is possible to have this *mushin* experience with God when practicing an art but then lose it when you move on to something else, just as we often feel Spirit in church but not at work. You have to maintain the same state of mind that makes this union possible in every activity or the connection vanishes. It is our discipline to tame the wild beast called the mind. It has ascended to a place that is not its true home. We must put it back where it belongs so that proper balance can be restored in the universe called yourself.

When this balance is achieved you will naturally respond to the myriad events of life in a manner appropriate to an awakened man. There will be no need for worry or second-guessing. Your faith in yourself will not be misplaced, because you will have uncovered the True Self, which is not the vain and petty man of ego, but the universal man God ordained to rule the earth. Each one of us is that universal personage but we have allowed a few people to control the world and our own head. The spiritual warrior knows that it is his duty to win honor and glory under his own name, for this is his just tribute to the One who made him. We will all be judged for what we did or don't do with the resources of self.

Let it not be said that you acquiesced to the loudest voice or denied your heritage because you listened to another man rather than to the Master within.

Sadly, that is indeed exactly what most men do. They have no hint of their true worth even though some call themselves the children of God. The spiritual warrior carries himself as a son of Heaven. He knows that he has an enemy who is also strong. The children of demons are evil and destructive; only the warrior armed with faith and courage will stand strong before them. There is only peace within the spiritual warrior, but the enemy attacks the body-mind. It is body and mind the spiritual warrior must protect. The enemy is also spiritual power operating in the realm of the physical. The warrior who stays focused in the Spirit through regular meditation and constant awareness can avoid dangers that others do not even sense.

We cannot continue to neglect our spiritual nature. Spirit is our life, although mind provides feedback and body is our form, our means of maintaining individuality. We must probe the depths of our being to come alive fully. Communication is by planes. Body to body is on the physical; mind to mind is on the intellectual; and spirit to spirit is beyond defining but not beyond experiencing. This is where Zen starts. That is to say, your movement and the existence of your being from the spiritual depths is what the ancients signified with the words Zen, Tao, saintliness, etc. So great is this way of life that those who have understood the possibilities have sacrificed all to seek it. We are not talking religion here, but a personal union, one on one with the source of your own being. This goes beyond the ability of any church, synagogue, or temple to share. This is a journey each man must take alone or not at all. The warrior and the saint travel a similar path; each must give his life if called for. Each must learn how to die in order to live.

As a warrior who began the Path in the Christian church, I never saw any reason to stop worshiping God in the same way as my fellow Christians, even though I later became a Zen-Dhyana Initiate. Church was my focus on God as being Supreme and Zen and the yogi paths reveal who I am as a single human being. The two do not conflict in any way when you actually practice. It is possible to live one's whole earthly life and never know what a human being (yourself) really is. That will mean most people die without ever getting a glimpse of their true selves. That suits the enemies of man just fine. To be restored to our original place in the scheme of the universe, Sunday spiritual training is not enough. There is no secular or spiritual division in enlightenment. Our whole being must be revitalized, and only the Masters of Masters can do that.

The One is within each of us. He has many names but He remains the same in all. The gurus call Him Lord, the Self of All. The Lord is One. It is taught that although He appears to men in different ways at different times in history, there is but One Lord manifesting to all according to their needs.

As you study the warrior art, understand that it

like all arts is a visible manifestation of an unseen path. The unseen, too, has its roots in a living reality. Trust yourself to this reality above reality. Do not try to explain it or understand it; simply use it. There is nothing to explain because by definition it is beyond defining. Accept the guidance of the Path and let life happen for you. Let the drama explode from the present with celestial excitement. Let your eyes return to their youthful glow as they behold the mystery. Life is a mystery even though we have words for just about everything. Do not take the words to be the Truth; they are just hints for what cannot be grasped by the mind. The spirit is already home, but it cannot speak the language of carnal mind; you must convert carnal mind to the image of spirit, clear, unbound, empty of concepts when it comes to the inner universe, when it comes to God. Only then can the Way appear with each step you take.

What is the proper way to block a sword thrust? When the enemy swings, only then is the path crystal clear. There is no path until there is a foot extended. This is the way of faith. If you can move without a plan, and act without thought, if you can believe that there is an Inner Master who can orchestrate the way you arrange flowers or play music or drive a car, then you are a spiritual warrior. Let go of yourself a little more each day and you will discover the matchless path of the Spirit and your real nature. Your lips will give forth wisdom and even children will sit at your feet in awe. Do these things and you will be as much an instrument of the Master as a horn is the instrument of a musician. Christ said, "The Father is in me and I am in you." *In you.* In many different languages and in many different ways the same message has been spoken in every culture. Lord Krishna says in the Bhagavagita, "I am the Me in all."

You have powers you know not of. So when you walk the streets in confidence that the Lord of the Universe is in your fingertips and stride, who can take you? Battles are won and lost in the mind. All is mind, say the Yogacara. Use yours for you. After all, we all have one; shouldn't yours be serving you?

Take back your mind from those who have mistaught you and re-examine your life and the universe around you. One hint—the sky is not above your head and there is no ground beneath your feet. If you attack me with a tank I will laugh in your face; its shells cannot find where I keep my heart. Ponder that and be free. If you are ever physically attacked by a larger enemy, clear your mind of any thought, clench your fist and charge forth like a bull elephant with all your might . . . or you could open your arms and say "Kill me," and smile.

FORM AND EMPTINESS

Form is form, emptiness is emptiness. Form is emptiness, emptiness is form, but still form is form and emptiness is emptiness. There is the apparent universe with all its trappings—we see it, hear it, smell it, and touch it; we even feel it, but there is more. That which is beyond our sensory perception is vast, mysterious, and awesome beyond our imagination, but not definable. Most men have a word for this—God. God is empty. That is, He takes up no space, or is all space; He defies the tools of science, yet He is the source of all being and intelligence. The masters of old learned to rely on emptiness as much as their conscious minds. They were raised to superior heights, but lowered themselves in humility in respect for the Source of their power.

In the West men try to understand everything, to reduce everything to a rational concept. They refuse to believe that there are experiences beyond the ability of their minds to grasp. As a result, they choose an intellectual construct over the Real. To experience oneness with God as He Himself desires us to, we must die to self and the ways of self. Worship and the arts are ways in which we can die to the small I and experience the Cosmic Mind. We must let God take over our education. The traditional Eastern approach differs from that of the West in that the artist or disciple of God seeks to merge with God so that his spirit flows into that of the Great Spirit. One device is the use of humility to empty himself of the false concept of an individual self. Another device is to defeat the image-generating habit of the mind by giving it nothing to focus on. If the mind has something to focus on it will produce a counterfeit version for the person to see. Emptiness gives no room for an image. Furthermore, by realizing that the mind cannot grasp ultimate reality in words, you defeat the talking mind. When the mind is brought to a state of stillness, then the matchless spiritual journey to Self begins in earnest. This is surrendering the will to the Unknown. It is the most frightening thought most Westerners can ever have, but this is the price everyone must pay to leap from the carnal (sentient) to the spiritual mind.

All of those who have blazed a path before us have declared that this sacrifice is well worth the fear it generates. A successful completion of this journey gives you a "heaven soaring" spirit which is clearly manifested in the everyday affairs of life. For the warrior, it gives him power over his body and circumstances. Body, mind, and spirit function as one. This oneness alone is a blessing to sing about for all of time.

Yet, when all is said and done, the spiritual warrior, the realized yogi, is nothing more than man as he is meant to function. Without unity within the self, how can there be unity in the world around us? We cannot predict what new circumstances will crop up every day, but if we are in spiritual oneness we know we can deal with whatever comes. We are always ready for action.

It is not enough to believe in yourself alone; there will come a day when even you will fail yourself. That is why we must also believe in a supportive power beyond our control—a safety net, a super intelligence—or there is no hope for the moment when all our strength is gone. Jesus said, "I will be with you even to the end of the world," assuring his disciples they were never alone. The Masters of the warrior arts stood beneath razor-sharp swords with supreme confidence because they were certain that Heaven would guide their blade.

I lived in New York City during the gang era. I have faced the possibility of death by violence many times. Heaven has always delivered me with grace, dignity, and style. Heaven will deliver you, if you embrace the Way with the spirit of your mind.

INTERNAL RADAR

A samurai always entered a room aware that the ceiling could fall at any minute. Expect the unexpected. Danger does not always come from another person; sometimes it comes from circumstances or inanimate objects. Once when I was riding a bus I noticed a lady with two infant children, one on her lap, one propped up beside her. I turned my attention back to my book. Moments later, the driver had to slam the brakes, and the seated child tumbled toward the floor. In an instant I let go of my book and lunged forward to catch the child. I caught him before he hit the floor. After handing the child to the grateful mother I picked up my book and began to read. Only then did I become aware of how fast and flawlessly I had moved. My movements were not conscious; had I thought through my movements the child would have hit the floor. By the time of the incident I was comfortable with the knowledge that my spirit had ability all its own for dealing with emergencies. The Inner

Master, the Unconscious, took control and saved the day. In my experience this level of activity is always suited to the circumstances.

Our eyes, ears, nose, and even skin are scanning devices for the spirit. If we use them without clinging to the information they provide, our spirit can freely act to the stimuli without stopping. As long as we have a mind to sift through information and block activity, we cannot reach the highest level of our being. When blocking ceases, the mind as we commonly think of it vanishes because there is no obstruction within it. Our actions then become spiritual—fluid and effortless. The warrior is always aware of his body in relationship to his environment. Body is what can be harmed by outside forces. He must learn to move in limited space and respond as needed.

It is important to be mindful of movement; that is, to be aware of your movement without trying to control it. As you appreciate the movement of your body, extend that awareness to your changing environment. If you are blind to the possibilities of danger, you will not signal yourself to be prepared for situations. There is no need to tell yourself how to act; it is enough to be aware that you may have to move at a moment's notice. Give yourself permission to act without thought.

Experienced drivers develop a type of automatic pilot that allows them to react quickly in an unexpected situation because anything can happen while driving. But anything can happen any time, any place. By extending your spirit into the surrounding world, you make your field of awareness greater without stress. As uncanny as it may seem, you are alert even during the hours of sleep. If something unusual happens you will awaken ready to take appropriate action. This is the kind of ability which lies beneath the ego-mind of every human being, the realm of self mastery.

The study we are advocating is one of unlearning rather than learning. Once man lost faith in his inherent wisdom we proceeded full speed down the path of accumulated knowledge. This is nothing like the path of wisdom where we began. Only by a willingness to let go, to drop back into the "empty" space we call the unknown can we begin to experience the true nature of the mind and find our own spiritual connection with everyday reality. In this way we join the dance of the universe as a participant, not as an observer. We become instruments of peace, love, and harmony. We naturally find the way to defend our peace and our love and maintain the harmony. It is not something that is seen as extra.

Our bodies are given to us for a time. We use them, but we are not them. They are finite and as subject to scrapes and bruises as our pets. We are responsible for protecting and taking care of them. If we view them as a precious treasure that is on loan to us, we will understand why we must guard them carefully. When we fail our bodies, we suffer emotionally and spiritually. They are like mediums through which our other natures interact. We may work on our bodies with our minds and vice versa, but our spiritual side must by nature find its root beyond our intellect, in God, that ground of all being which cannot be grasped at all by intellect.

The free movement of the Art of Dancing to No-Music is one way of teaching your body to respond to the spontaneous signals of the spirit. This is not unlike Tai Chi, but without the fixed forms. In dancing you give free reign to your own spiritual connection rather than follow a pattern set by another. Patience is required. I'll give you some guidelines to get you started.

Dancing to No-Music

Creativity comes from an untraceable place. We do it best when we accept it and use it. The Art of Dancing to No-Music is a martial dance. As the practitioner you assume the posture and attitude of defense, but you consider no movement. There is no tension in the body. You hold the posture and meditate on your position. Your mind is in a state of surrender. You have a beginner's mind, like a child who is open to learning and being guided. Concentrate on feeling with the essence of your being, not on thought. When you are really relaxed, your back straight, your weight distributed evenly, you will notice that your body will start to move on its own. Flow with it. Follow the movement of your hands, the swivelling of your body whenever it wants to go without interpretation. In this manner, you are training your body and mind to be responsive to your spirit. This is a method I use to cultivate *aiki*, spiritual harmony.

VERNON KITABU TURNER

By practicing the Art of Dancing to No-Music I am keenly aware of the difference between the movement of my body as directed by conscious mind and the movement of my body as directed by Spirit. There is no comparison. The spiritual movement is without any effort at all. It is serene and sweet to experience. I am aware that I am connected to that which is greater than I—something which leads me to correct action. I called that something the Creator, or God. David referred to the same power as the Lord of his strength in Psalm 144. We are not talking about something that is peculiar to Asian masters but a possibility open to any human being who seeks it. The trigger which opens the gate to this power is faith. As said many, many times before, spiritual power or realization cannot be accessed by intellect. There are real and measurable results we experience in our bodies and through our actions, but the leap to this level of activity is not through knowledge. By letting go and feeling the free movement of your body as it takes meaningful form without your conscious demand, you see for yourself that there is another level of intelligent presence within you capable of taking charge. Through this practice we learn to yield to the Way of the Master in other areas of our lives. This is practice . . . a practical application of what most people accept in their religion as true. It is the difference between belief and actualizing one's belief. By practice, we can live in the Spirit of the Master for all to see. We practice to become one with the power. We become the manifestation. People experience the truth through our presence and activity.

113

By Dancing to No-Music we learn to follow the inner music which connects us with our origin. No external person can guide you on this path and you cannot find it by imitating others. The secret of your uniqueness lies within you. Only you can discover the path which leads you home. If you discover that path you will become a star wherever you happen to be. A star is one of a kind. It has its own light in the heavens. Dance to generate that light within, which will guide you safely through this world of would-be clones. Ride the Creator's wave that is the real you to self-mastery, and every challenge will be another opportunity to learn the secret of what man truly is.

THE ENEMY

The spiritual warrior has no enemy but himself. The contest is always against oneself. You cannot control how others will act toward you but you can govern your own actions and reactions. O Sensei Uyeshiba reminds us that the true art of the warrior is to receive the spirit of the universe and to spread his peace. His definition of the Way of the Warrior is love.

When I began my study of the Way of the Warrior I wanted to know how to defend myself from outside threats and to protect my loved ones. There was never a desire to be the aggressor. As a young Christian boy I chose El Shaddai, the Mighty Conqueror, the Lord of Hosts, as my *sensei*. Sometimes He sent me human teachers, other times I learned from plants and animals. Through the lessons I came to experience to a greater degree than ever before the virtue of the spiritual route of study. Direct perception of truth is superior to all secondary forms of education. Only direct perception leads to enlightenment. Accumulated information creates only an imitation of the real thing.

I respect the Aikido of Uyeshiba because he discovered his art by direct spiritual perception. He wanted to lead his students to do the same . . . to tap the spiritual resource within their own being. Unfortunately, many of current descendants only imitate his techniques, failing to grasp the spirit of the art. When one embraces the spirit of love and peace there is no room for an enemy within your mind. The concept of enemy is unnecessary to the spirit of defense. If a force attacks you from outside, you will deal with the threat accordingly without losing your peace, if you practice maintaining spiritual harmony. The Aikido of Uyeshiba Sensei is also a dance. It is Uyeshiba's dance. The Art of Dancing to No-Music is my dance, but the insight of both arts are founded on a common reality. They reveal the nature of our spirits in action. A musician creates better when he channels his spirit through his instruments without worry about competition from other musicians. In like manner, a warrior is at his greatest when he channels his spirit through his body without concern for the antics of the enemy because the spirit acts independently of external phenomena. The spiritual warrior has only to trust himself wholly to the spirit.

Through such tests as battle or confrontation, the spiritual warrior learns to conquer his mind and give way to the spirit. This is the transition from carnal mindedness—that is, the mind that is flesh-centered—to spiritual mindedness, the mind that is focused on spirit. The arts of Asia are practiced as tools of forging spiritual strength. To master the warrior's art, the student must do constant battle with his own mind. The mind does not see the world as it is; nor does it perceive the true self. It knows only what it has been taught by outsiders, none of whom were enlightened to the true nature of their own mind and spirit. When the warrior brings the beast that is his own mind under control he will see and hear clearly. He will be like a newborn baby, but filled with wisdom rather than awe. The secret of what man is, that creation said to be created in the likeness of God, is in you. If you cannot lay claim to the awesome truth, no one can. The warrior entered a battle knowing that he must wield his own weapon or perish. Life is like that. You must learn to uncover the secret of your own power if you are to live the life of a champion. The spiritual warrior is a student of the Ultimate Teacher. The Ultimate Teacher who is at once the Inner Master and the outward manifestation men call Lord teaches us to be the best we can be, to always reach higher into the heavens. Only men would limit us for their own selfish gain.

The physical struggles we face each day are only outward signs of a spiritual war that goes on day after day. There are only two sides in a war. There is no middle ground. Because there is no middle ground the warriors on either side do not need to hesitate when they clash. The war is constant . . . straight on until the end. Hesitation is doubt. Doubt leads to failure or death.

A warrior once asked a Zen Master how he

should face battle. "Hold your sword high and charge into battle without looking back," he said. From the cradle to the grave we will face opposition of all sorts. The successful student of life will keep his eye singularly focused on the star—the Master—as his goal and charge into the daily battle wielding his mind as a sword of the Spirit. Only the surrendered mind makes a gleaming sword which can move this way and that without effort. Whether facing a physical threat or a spiritual one, the spiritual warrior knows that the whole battle is really fought within his own mind. He is not deceived into hating his fellow man, for he knows that the roots of all men begin and end in the same place. The spiritual warrior serves the Master by becoming a soldier of humanity, a defender of the weak. Yield and overcome.

THE ART OF LIFE AND DEATH

Long before you face a physical foe in battle, you must learn to accept the great enemy—death. Physical life is impermanent, as we all know; it cannot be clung to indefinitely. The spiritual warrior practices surrendering his hold on physical life, day by day. As long as our mind is focused on our flesh as ourselves we will harbor fear which will cause us to hesitate and make grave errors doing times of crisis. The carnal mind is our enemy. The spiritual mind is life. The warrior must never forget that his body is no more than a pile of animated dust which is significant only because his spirit quickens it. It is his duty to become intimate with his spirit. He does so by yielding the movements of his body and the direction of his mind to the wisdom of the spirit. Human beings seem to forget that they, too, are spirits. They are so wrapped up in the material they lose sight of the true. The material world could vanish in a heartbeat. Nothing of the physical world will cross the great void of death. The saints, even Joan of Arc, have shown us that death should be faced bravely.

They were able to accept their fate because they were aware of a higher reality than flesh and blood.

To be accepting of death does not mean throwing your life away or giving yourself to be destroyed. When the fear of death is removed from your consciousness, only then can you be fully alive to the moment and the possibilities. Duality vanishes and you can act freely. There is a Zen saying: Only that which is born can die . . . only the body is born.

The warrior faces the possibility of death at any moment; it is for that reason that the Warrior Path is a good metaphor for the spiritual student. We do not know how long we will be on this earth. We need to make that transition from carnal to spiritual while we can. The sword of the enemy called death could strike at any moment. God is spirit. He communes only with spirit. Only when we answer the call of the Spirit and become quickened in our own spirits can we become students of the Master. Make no mistake, there is but one Master who reaches out to quicken the minds and spirits of humans. He may use whatever form He desires to instruct, whether human, mineral, or animal, but He is the same Holy Spirit who spoke through the prophets and fought through the warriors and sang through the musicians down through the ages. He is our teacher who leads us into all mysteries, if we seek Him. The Inner Master is perfect, flawless in instruction. To those who seek His guidance in earnest, He will come. He may be that stranger in the night, a preacher or a transient, but if you have learned to tap your own spirit, you will know the Spirit, by the Spirit. The humble student of the Warrior Way will seek help first from the Inner Master, then human help will come according to the need. The outer teacher will always confirm what you have received in secret, or he is not of that spirit. There are secular ways of doing everything. The spiritual way is called the Way of Heaven because only when you abandon the way of self, it comes . . . and it comes from within.

Finally, if we learn to seek out our spiritual nature by yielding our mind to the Spirit, we will discover peace and the power of love as we have never known them before. Our arts will come with greater ease and we will be attuned to the dance of life all around us. This is the path illuminated by Jesus when he said, "Not my will but thy will be done." We think that the way we use our minds now is good, but our minds have been distorted through the ages. We do not know the Original Mind. Only by surrendering our ego-self to the Most High, Unfathomable God, have men become enlightened . . . free. Only these men can laugh at the great storms of life and travel the endless reaches of the universe with ease. Worship is praise and fellowship; our arts provide a way of realization, one-on-one perception which shows itself in our daily life. The war is raging every day. Are you man or woman enough to challenge your own ego-centered mind to battle? The prize is so great words cannot convey its measure. When you have learned to battle this great enemy to even a draw, no outside opponent will stand a chance against you. This is the way to mastery.

MO CHI CHU:
PRESSING ON TO THE MARK

It is the duty of every person born to advance to the highest level of life he or she is capable of. That means we should first set our mark on spiritual goals. Spiritual power will manifest in every walk of life, even the material, but material goals will not of themselves aid us in spiritual growth. By spiritual we mean inner development. We need to keep our mind's eye centered on the Master, or his designate. The designate would be any teacher who reflects the spirit of the Master; that teacher is an extension of the One. As the moon reflects the light of the sun but claims no light of his own, so also do the spiritual Masters on earth reflect the light of the True Son who shines within us all. Spirituality illuminates the dark recesses of our mind and restores our ability to learn directly from the universe about the true nature of ourselves.

The path of the warrior and any student of life is straight ahead. We advance each day toward the end of our journey on Earth, but have we ascended to the higher road? When the warrior keeps the person of the Master in line with his spiritual vision, he is always moving toward higher ground in his reaction toward the experiences of life. The Master says, "Come to me," though the path is a treacherous one. The warrior must draw his sword and pass through this valley of death with his head held high, as befitting a student of the Master. He must press on toward the mark no matter what tries to stop him. Faith can be proven only by taking action. The Master represents our own spiritual connection with God. Our mind has blocked this connection from our awareness. In order for us to reclaim our living connection we must defeat our primary enemy. That enemy is the mind and all its illusions that are cast as monsters, demons, and warriors in our daily path. The Master says we can pass through them without being harmed, but they are fierce to behold. Which do we believe, our eyes or the Master, Himself? Those who follow the Master do not travel by sight but by faith, faith in the promise of the spirit within us. Only by accepting life's challenges and defeating the voice of reason can we walk on water and raise the dead. Our sentient (carnal) mind is death. Only the empty (spiritual) mind is life.

A Zen student faced a dilemma. He was poised on the edge of a cliff when his beloved Master said, "Walk on." What should he do when walking on means death? If you have faith in the promise of the Master you will choose what appears to be death rather than losing faith in Him. Nothing is what it appears to be, but you will never know the truth of your life until you take risk in the name of the Master.

In the West most worshipers of God believe that

God speaks through their ministers. They have no problem with that concept. Yet they do not understand the role of a Master or a teacher as do those in the East. As the preacher preaches by virtue of the Holy Spirit, the Master lives and teaches by virtue of the same Holy Spirit. His job is not to convince the student of the existence of God or things spiritual; those who come to him already have such an experience. The teacher's job is to help the student make the transition from his carnal nature to a complete spiritual awakening. When this happens, the student acts from his spirit, not from his body-mind. Spirit is life-affirming; it is life itself. In such a person, all of his activities flow from his spiritual insight and the world is turned upside-down. His relationship with the Creator is oneness. This is the childlike trust to which Jesus Christ alluded when he said, "Come as a child." The hardest thing for the Western mind to do is to relinquish its own self-centeredness and fall into the abyss with only faith.

But spiritual mastery means letting go of everything, giving yourself nothing to hold on to at all. Without prior proof, the warrior or student of the Spirit must fall into emptiness because he has faith that the Master will manifest at the critical moment and save the day. He acts because he loves the Master more than life itself and does not fail to follow his inner guidance. This faith manifests as arts and inspired movement. The same power which created the universe and all life moves within the disciple; the creation continues through him. For the joy of being an instrument in the hands of the Master of Masters, the spiritual warrior and the saint risk all their earthly possessions, even their lives.

For the warrior, going ahead means never hesitating to meet his enemies in battle, if he is called to fight. He must pass on through even if it seems that death is eminent. He knows that the Master stands on the other shore with His arms outstretched to welcome him, if he should be cut down. But, if he were to cower and surrender to preserve his physical life a few days longer, it signifies spiritual defeat. The saint, too, must be willing to surrender his physical life in the cause of the Master, should he be called upon to stand for right in the face of the enemy.

Since in a war there are only two sides, and nothing permitted in the middle, the warrior and the saint know that if they are under attack they must resist with all their might. They know who the enemy is and that he will never cease to press for their destruction. The enemy has no mercy for human beings, especially spiritual ones. With this in mind, the warrior is vigilant. He knows that life calls for his all, for he is in a battle for his soul at all times. The enemy may manifest as a mugger or a thief or a soldier in a political war, but the goal is the same—to destroy and conquer.

The warrior defends himself against physical assault, mental attackers, and, lastly, his own mind. His own mind is his greatest enemy because of its subtle role. It stands as a barrier against spiritual expression. It must be defeated in order for you, as spirit, to emerge from captivity. That is why the Masters refer to the mind as No Mind. When it functions as it should, there is no tension or division to alert us of its presence. The spiritual mind is vast and empty, crystal clear waters which accurately reflect the spiritual origin of man.

Meeting the mind head-on in battle is the most important job of the warrior or saint. The mind suppresses your true identity and blocks your power as a man. You were free as a child until adults trained your mind to believe in the world of form to the degree it lost its fluidity. Now only by cutting this mind off at the roots will you be able to release the awesome power and grace of your spirit.

Each one of us is one. We are independently connected to the universe and are spiritual offspring of God. However, we have been taught to see ourselves as part of a group or groups. This is false perception. We each came here alone. We each return alone. The journey through life is a lonely spiritual one, but we are fooled by the mind to follow the crowd. We will never understand who we are that way. We must trace the spiritual roots which pass within us, connecting our life to the mind of the Creator is order to be fully alive as He intends. The mind is a separate entity which draws us into the life of the universe, the material plane, but it does not recognize or know anything about the spiritual path. What it surmises is illusion. The spiritual path is not the path of knowledge but of acceptance.

If you as a spiritual warrior are in a battle, your hands and feet would move of their own accord. If you were meant to be a man of peace, you would instantly know how to respond in peace, without thought. The spiritual path does not rely on thought or deliberation of any kind. It is action which is one with all wisdom. This is the reward which is given to them who love the Unknown, Unknowable God. This is how they become "sons of God." In the Orient, the warriors schooled in the inner-school are called the "sons of heaven." There is no greater experience in life.

Lesser men value knowledge, the accumulation of facts and figures one at time. By learning in this way they may praise themselves for their accomplishments. The spiritual warrior acts from the same power which created him. He knew nothing at birth, yet he breathed and moved and was aware. He returns to this state of mind and finds that the world becomes clear, his mind receptive to the vibrations of life all around. This mind does not block information but receives all with the receptivity of the ears and the eyes and other senses. Such a man is aware that his life flows from the mysterious source. He takes nothing and no one for granted. He sees the supernatural in the most common occurrence; the seen and the unseen come together in him to form the dance of life, of which he is an intimate part. The warrior, no less than the saint or artisan, should apply himself to the highest study so that body, mind, and spirit harmonize in the proper order. When this happens, the life of the world around becomes filled with the vibrations of heaven; personal bliss is heaven's reward for your breaking through to the supreme highway.

BOW TO THE MASTER: THE POWER OF HUMILITY

In The East we pay homage to our Lord and Master by demonstrating our humility before Him. We bow. We do not *say* we are humble; we show it. Bowing is the lowering of body-mind. Both the body and mind function in the material universe. We bow to yield that part of ourselves which is in the world to Him who created the worlds. As we yield we empty ourselves of ego, leaving a space which can be filled by the Spirit of Truth. The more we bow and practice yielding, the stronger the power of the Spirit in us. The Master Spirit quickens our spirit. We become alive to our true nature. By becoming alive to our spiritual nature we are guided through this world of mind and matter, a world full of illusion and traps for our souls. The warrior pledges his loyalty to a master, either a secular leader or a spiritual one. This pledge determines the direction of his mind. He must have a cause for which to direct his energy.

It is the battle which follows which sharpens his skills and proves his mettle.

The directive power comes from the Master within, the Lord. It may be channeled through a human Master who is already one with his spiritual nature. When the warrior pledges himself to the cause of the Master he yields himself to the will of his leader, thus becoming an extension of the Master Himself. Even an army of warriors have but one mind, the mind of the commander. The well-functioning army functions as one with the leader. The Master gives focus to the warrior.

By bowing to the Master before you practice your art or arts and acknowledging His presence within, you keep your mind focused on the highest spiritual goal at all times. Your mind and body will become aligned as one with the Spirit in time, and you will be able to travel through the by-ways of life responding to life and events with spontaneous wisdom. This has been the experience of countless Masters through the ages and in all cultures. God is One. It is He who has established the arts and the system of Masters to help us reach our potential. The Way of the Masters is different from worship of God in a church or similar institution. Worship in a church is a group effort. The Way of the Masters is to enter the kingdom within you, to pass beyond the mind and body and become spirit. This is the goal of religion as well. The only way this task can be completed is alone. We must use whatever tool is at hand to defeat the false perceptions of mind to restore our oneness with ourselves as enjoyed in childhood. The scriptures tell us that if we succeed in that mission we will reach the kingdom of heaven, the kingdom of the Spirit. The Asiatic countries have excelled in such spiritual disciplines aimed at bringing the mind in subjection to the spirit. Zen and yoga are two such approaches. Yoga focuses on God and the lore of saints to stir faith and bring the mind into focus on the Lord. Zen transcends all references and gives the mind nothing to grab hold of, not even itself. In the Zen approach, the false mind is made to collapse under its own weight. The Zen mind-spiritual mind manifests on its own, instinctively wise, instinctively correct. It knows nothing of its origin; it simply is, functioning in harmony with the world around.

By seeking refuge within the self as both the Buddha and Jesus Christ advocated, we find our true home. From the safety of this place we are able to live and work in this world without being of it. We become the center of the universe . . . the still point. Everything we see, hear, taste, and touch—and even those things which are not of sight and sound—are part of our experience of life. As we yield, humbly, we become a student of everyday life with our whole being. To learn what we are, we must be willing to be all alone. We learn how the other people in the world fit into the puzzle of life. Our arts and skills become expressions of the Creator within us. We are part of his ebb and flow. For this reason we have arts and opposition, so that we might learn to rely on the unseen for our guidance and thus become co-creators with the Supreme Lord in the ever-expanding story of the universe. Every man and woman born can become a reflection of God by searching within, not for answers to words but in order to let go of everything but Him. Only when we do so do we discover the power of oneness. There is only one you. In life you will meet friends and foes; you must know how to handle both. If you consolidate your power within you, you will always act appropriate to the needs of the moment. There is nothing to learn. Take your mind back from the world of knowledge and find your roots in God or No-thing. One day your mind will return to its proper place. There will be a flash of light and your soul will be your shimmering sword. Remember, the same power which wiggles your finger so easily can be the secret of your success in all other areas of this life. It came with you in birth, it will go with you in death. Find its source now while you are still alive and even death will have no victory over you. You may not understand this, but you yourself are the house of the rising sun. Walk boldly though this life . . . be number one, a reflection of the Master.

EPILOGUE

"A Mind Like Water"

conversations with Vernon Kitabu Turner
(Interview by Simeon Alev from
What Is Enlightenment magazine)

Part I: Introduction

"Yeah, I know Vernon," said the voice on the other end of the line.

I was talking with Detective Willie Mills of the Portsmouth, Virginia, police department's Crime Prevention Unit, a martial artist and former student of the renowned jujitsu master C. O. Neal. Until I'd managed to get Detective Mills on the phone, I'd been batting zero. Now I was excited. Mills had witnessed, over twenty-four years ago, the legendary public spectacle in which a fresh-faced young poet named Vernon Kitabu Turner had accepted challenges from top martial artists throughout the metropolitan region known as Hampton Roads—and defeated each of them in a matter of seconds. And even more amazing and mystifying than the haste with which Turner had dispatched his dangerous opponents was the way he was alleged to have done it: With one finger!

I apologized to Detective Mills for sounding skeptical. I'd already spent a beautiful day visiting with the extraordinarily gentle Turner in downtown Norfolk the week before, and trying to verify his out-rageous claims after the fact was making me feel vaguely guilty.

"You don't have to apologize to me," said Mills. "I'm a policeman. I check everything out. I'd be checking him out if I were you."

I admitted I was having a difficult time visualiz-ing Turner's one finger technique.

"Have you ever seen someone get stabbed? It's hard to see what's going on—kind of like two people dancing," Mills explained. "The knife does all the work. It don't look like much—but it's very detri-mental."

"Oh," I said, still finding it hard to imagine Turner wreaking such invisible havoc on his oppo-nents, particularly since he himself had told me that his victims feel no pain, sustain no injuries and never inspire anything but love in his heart.

"Well," said the Detective, "Vernon does have an unusual skill. Unusual—but not unheard of. It's called 'a mind like water,' and if you're just learning about all this for the first time, then you're about to embark on a fascinating journey."

As I reflected on the day I'd spent with Vernon Turner, I realized that it had indeed been only a beginning, and that for some mysterious reason, Turner—not only his incredible feats but the man himself—remained in some ways as much of an enigma after our meeting as he had been before I'd flown to Virginia, half expecting to be greeted at the airport by a larger-than-life hybrid of *Kung Fu's* Kwai Chang Caine and Superman. If everything I'd read about him was true, I'd mused that day on the plane, then Vernon Turner was indeed the closest thing to an authentic superhero I was ever likely to meet. . . . Vernon Kitabu Turner was born in Portsmouth in 1948, and as he drove me to my hotel from Norfolk Airport this past September, his descriptions of the neighborhoods and landmarks passing by outside my window recalled the trials and indignities of his boyhood in a segregated South—"during a time," he reminded me later, "when black people had no enforceable rights and our lives were cheap." It was under these circumstances that he had vowed, at the age of nine, "to become the protector of the weak," giving himself to the art of self-defense "with no less devotion than the samurai of Japan." This was a big decision for a bookish weakling who, because of his long, unaccountable silences and a peculiar sense of detachment from his own body, had always been considered "weird" by his family and friends.

Turner was first introduced to the late Master

Neal, who maintained a dojo [martial arts school] in his neighborhood, when he was twelve years old and something of a prodigy. Neal recognized the boy's potential, but Turner chose not to study with him, maintaining instead a close but informal relationship with the well-known teacher while practicing on his own and devising workouts from the ancient Japanese martial arts manuals he'd discovered at the public library. (It was in one such text that he first learned of Bushido, the way of inner cultivation.) Then, at the age of seventeen, after having spent nearly two years in the hospital with tuberculosis, Turner left Virginia for New York City where, armed only with the phone number of a friend of his mother's, he began a new life in the gang-ridden Bedford-Stuyvesant section of Brooklyn. Within weeks of his arrival, he told me, he'd already begun to fulfill his childhood promise, earning a reputation in the streets of an unfamiliar city for his bold willingness to stand up to "practitioners of violence and other forms of stupidity."

During his time in New York, Turner completed high school and college and worked as a writer and editor, contributing his literary and theatrical skills to the burgeoning Black Arts movement. He also had several unusual and seemingly coincidental encounters with itinerant spiritual teachers from the Near and Far East, the most powerful of which was his fateful meeting with the Zen master Nomura Roshi in 1967. In his book *Soul Sword*, Turner writes: "Family problems triggered emotional conflict that gave me no peace. Then one day after praying for guidance or relief, I was led by the spirit within me to travel twenty-five miles to Greenwich Village. I met a man, dressed in a kimono, sitting with folded hands on a bench in Washington Square Park. The air around him was charged with peace. I was in bliss in his presence."

Turner had been meditating, by his own estimation, since he was three years old and had always felt isolated from others and unsure of his place in the world because of his inward-directed and deeply spiritual nature. In the presence of Nomura Roshi, who had just arrived from Japan the day before, Turner received instant confirmation of his own experience and promptly accepted him as his teacher. "After being initiated into the way of *zazen* [meditation] by the Master," he writes, "I continued to practice martial arts and do *shikantaza* [formless meditation] as if there were no relationship between the two. Imagine how surprised I was when one day as I sat in meditation there was a melting away of barriers, a blaze of light, and I immediately understood the secret of self-defense from the inside out. There was no mystery. When I arose from my seat, I felt as if everything was clear to me." With virtually no formal training in the martial arts, the youthful Vernon Turner had apparently—in "a blaze of light"— become a master.

I already knew the story's ending. Turner had spent the next several months seeking out martial arts masters willing to put his realization to the test—and meeting every challenge. Then, when he returned to Virginia, his old friend Master Neal arranged a "trial by combat" through the Board of United Dojo Organizations (BUDO), "a council sanctioned by the highest-ranking sensei [teachers] and masters in Hampton Roads." Turner was pitted against "seasoned black belts, at one point against six black belts at the same time." At the end of his ordeal, the council met. "Thanks to the graciousness of the masters and the direction of my Inner Master, I made the leap from no formal rank to black belt and fourth degree in Wa-Jitsu (The Way of Accord) and Aikijutsu, and was awarded the Ronin (masterless warrior) Award by the council." Soon after this, Turner had the most decisive encounter of his life. He met his beloved Indian guru, Sant Keshavadas, who recognized him as a spiritual teacher in his own right and blessed his mission to "heal the African American soul."

As we continued to make our way downtown, I found myself becoming more and more eager to begin our interview. My "traveler's mind" had settled down, coming to rest on the challenging questions that had brought me here. What was the "secret" that the soft-spoken man sitting next to me had understood? Was it enlightenment? And if so, what was its relationship to a mastery of self so consummate that within days of his revelation he had been willing to submit it to such a grueling series of ultimate tests?

As I recalled the superhero images that Turner's prose had inspired in my mind, I also couldn't help but wonder how closely the impeccable, divinely inspired warrior who had written his way into my imagination would prove to resemble the flesh-and-blood human being with whom I was about to spend the afternoon. For while I had little doubt that Turner's epic journey was as authentic as it was amazing, I could never entirely forget that I was in the presence of a talented poet who, blessed with the heart of Odysseus and the tongue of Homer, might have been tempted by the muse at every turn to take part in the creation of his own legend.

The essence of Turner's attainment, as he himself describes it, is the realization of "no-self," the experiential understanding that he is "but an instrument, grass blown by the wind: the grass is taking the bows but the wind is doing all the work." He is adamant in his unwillingness to accept credit for his accomplishments—much as he clearly enjoys talking about them—and relentless in his insistence that his actions are solely manifestations of "the Spirit, the Lord God, Ultimate Truth." And in fact, in the course of our short journey together, I'd already developed the distinct impression that there are two Vernon Kitabu Turners: one, a bemused and humble observer of human nature, and the other—fleetingly revealed by the sidelong glances I occasionally cast in his direction—a genuinely powerful and far more mysterious presence that seems to transcend the confines of any isolated human personality. Even when we were face to face, I was to witness this extraordinary alternation countless times, eventually with a frequency that made it all but impossible to doubt Turner's assessment of his own experience. For all of his vaunted ability, the force that animated this unusual man appeared to be that of being itself or, as he preferred to call it, "Not I." And for all of his many triumphs, the essence of his victory appeared to be surrender to a power far greater than his own. "The Unborn," he writes, "the mind like water, is real only to those who can experience it as a living reality. To attempt to grasp it as an intellectual concept is to murder it. . . . When I stand on the mat rooted in the grace of this awesome experience and see my opponents fly through the air and fall at my feet without conscious effort on my part, when I feel my body rise and fall like the cosmic breath, I am humbled by life. I realize that somehow, mysteriously, I am a partaker of something greater than I can comprehend."

Turner is well aware, he told me, that the depth of his absorption in the forces that guide the universe will probably never be more than a bizarre and purely hypothetical notion to Westerners who view self-mastery as the apotheosis of autonomy and control. "But this is because," he says, "they fail to listen. If we allow it to be, there is an indomitable spirit present within all of us or no one would have it." And he is also aware that those who are impressed by his feats in the ring would probably find his susceptibility to spontaneous meditation more difficult to appreciate. "I'll give you a recent example," he told me as, ensconced in my hotel room, we were about to begin our interview. "I was sitting in Dunkin' Donuts holding a cup of coffee, and when I looked up, there was a policeman standing in front of me.

"So I said, 'Yes, Officer? May I help you?'

"'Is everything okay?' he asked.

"'Well, yes,' I said. 'What's wrong with drinking a cup of coffee?'

"'*Nothing* is wrong with drinking a cup of coffee,' he told me. 'It's just that you've been looking at that cup *for the past eight hours*.'

"I thought to myself, 'Oh, my God. Eight hours have gone by. I'm in a public place. People are working here. They've been watching me, but I haven't been aware of them at all.' And then I said to myself, 'Vernon, you'd better be careful, because you're not in Asia, where they understand these things. You're in the U.S. of A.—where they definitely don't.'"

Part II: The Interview

WIE: What, in your view, is the relationship between enlightenment and self-mastery?

Vernon Turner: Well, enlightenment is first of all coming to understand that there is no self in the conventional sense. People tend to think of the self as, "Well, I'm the guy who went to this high school and had these parents, and I'm the guy who's got an accounting degree, and I worked my way through it all and achieved these things." Now that's purely an illusory self that we're talking about. Enlightenment is coming to understand or experience that there is no objective self—there is a being, but there's no objective self—and it's in the process of letting go of that notion that one experiences what one truly is in the universal sense. That's when enlightenment comes—when you realize that you are not in control. And because of that, you are very much in control.

WIE: And how would you distinguish that from self-mastery?

VT: Well, the difference may be more in terms of language than reality because enlightenment is the opening up of the eye of perception to the ultimate reality of existence itself. But on the finite scale the application would be self-mastery. In the enlightenment aspect of it there's no one there: There is no you to operate as opposed to this person or that person; your experience is complete, it's whole, it contains the cosmos. But when this enlightenment expresses itself in form, as in walking down the street, speaking and carrying oneself, then its light shines through the eyes of a single entity, and that is when it is known as "self-mastery."

WIE: Do you think that perhaps the distinction may also go deeper than that? The reason I ask is because conventionally, self-mastery is associated with the achievement of a powerful and overwhelmingly positive sense of self, and certainly a very clear notion of oneself—an identity—while enlightenment, even when it is manifested in the world of time and space, is traditionally understood much as you have described it: as the dissolution, or the transcendence, of any separate sense of self, be it positive or negative.

VT: When an enlightened person is still, that's enlightenment, but the moment they move, it becomes, as I said, self-mastery, because the moment you move, you have to act in the world of particulars—you have to walk, talk, work, do all these things. Now people who observe your ability to function in this world are going to see you in this heightened state of reality; they're going to see the way you carry yourself and they're going to attribute extraordinary things to you. The point is, though, that in enlightenment you wouldn't necessarily attribute these things to yourself, and that's the main difference. But also, the enlightenment experience doesn't apply to anything in particular, whereas self-mastery can be divided into certain fields. So you could have mastery in many different fields, and yet, even with that mastery, not be enlightened in the true sense.

WIE: Someone like Anthony Robbins might be an interesting example in this context because what he teaches—theoretically anyway—would seem to transcend the parameters of any particular field. We're talking in this case about an individual who presents himself as, and who to all appearances seems to be, the master of himself.

And it would seem to be the case that whatever he's got, whatever realization he's had, covers very systematically every aspect of his life and, as far as he's concerned, of life in general. That's more the kind of mastery that I'm interested in trying to distinguish from enlightenment. Would you say that someone like Anthony Robbins is enlightened? Or is there an attainment that lies beyond the kind of self-mastery that he has achieved?

VT: No, I would not say that's enlightenment. I would say that Robbins has an uncanny ability to master through emulation, to model that which already exists. It's like two people who play a musical instrument: One has studied at Juilliard, but the other one has the gift; he can just pick up the instrument and start playing. Of course the other one can play too—he just picks up a sheet of music and starts playing. Well, most people would say that the guy who got his degree from Juilliard is a superior player because he's got his degree.

But in reality the person who gets his inspiration directly from the source is the superior one because he doesn't get it in a secondary way. We human beings have the ability to pick things up from each other—we do that in the first grade, we do it from our mother when we learn how to talk, and Dr. Shinichi Suzuki used the same method when teaching children how to play violin.

So Anthony Robbins has learned what triggers that response, a like response, and has been able to pass that secret on to a lot of people. But enlightenment is not about being able to perform tricks like that, you know? It's beyond that because it's all pervasive, and it's beyond any particular ability because it encompasses all abilities. From my point of view, everybody is playing the music, everybody is building the houses, everybody is putting together computers and all these things. They're all "me" in the first place—I have all those abilities—even though they're not all "Vernon Kitabu Turner." It's just that since I have many bodies, I don't have to do all those things in this body because one body over here is working on this part and another body over there is working on that part, and I'm reaping the fruits of it because I'm sitting here in a hotel that I did not personally build. But man built it. And because man built it, yes, I did build it, because I'm man!—I mean, who else could I be? So in that sense, enlightenment is the wholeness of what we are; it's understanding and appreciating the essence of what man is.

There's a scripture that asks the question, "What is man that thou art mindful of him?" In other words, "What is man in his essential nature?" And the particular expression of that would be, "What are you doing with this same ability and power?" Well, I can feel that essence coming through you in your work and appreciate and know it for what it really is—a part of ourselves—and I can appreciate the same thing in another person as something else. And when I express that essence, for me it is being able to flow with everything, knowing that there is nothing else but this, letting it flow through this body, act through this body, be this body wholly without having to look to the left, look to the right, ask permission from anybody because it's all me, and I'm giving my whole self to it.

WIE: So practically speaking, the difference between the kind of mastery that I've used Robbins to exemplify and the condition of an enlightened individual would be—

VT: That the enlightened being encompasses all beings in one, while mastery is focused only on the individual being. So if you're a master flycaster, you know that I'm not getting any fish on my end because I can't even get the fly to go on the water right. You have mastered that body. But if I'm going to do that myself, I'm going to have to apply myself as you have, learn the techniques that are necessary to gain mastery over that particular field—or whatever field.

WIE: No matter how total or comprehensive that field might be.

VT: Right, because even then we're still talking about mastering that field and then applying it to a particular goal or a particular life. Enlightenment is not a form of mastery in that sense, because in order for there to be a form of mastery, there has to be someone who's standing above it, and if you're already everything, then how could you stand above it, you see? If you're already everything, then why would you need mastery?

WIE: The martial arts, though, would also seem to represent a particular form of mastery, and yet you've described them as a path to enlightenment. What is it that makes the martial arts a path to transcendence, or the experience of "no-self," rather than simply another powerful means of developing one's strength, one's skill, one's mastery or sense of personal accomplishment?

VT: It can be approached from both directions. The average person who studies martial arts today, and even those in ancient periods, did so because they wanted to have physical strength in order to be able to subdue an enemy or protect themselves, or to have a sense of personal power. And there was also the aspect of being aggressive or warlike as a way of earning one's living, and in that case it was a career. But then, on the other hand, you had the spiritual people. People forget that Bodhidharma, the twenty-eighth patriarch of the Buddha, was the one who introduced the foundation of what is known as Shaolin Kung Fu today. On his way to China he became aware of the dangers on the road from robbers who would try to attack him in order to get the very important records that he carried. So he meditated, and it was revealed to him to study the animals, and in time he developed what came to be called the "Eighteen Movements of Lo Han." And these Eighteen Movements evolved into Shaolin Kung Fu and inspired many other martial arts after that.

The idea was that a person who is working for the good of humanity does not develop an aggressive nature but a peaceful center, and his purpose is to defend, not to attack—to defend his own body, to defend loved ones, to defend those who are weaker than himself, and never to desire to do harm even to the one who is attacking you, never to allow yourself to become like the evil ones who would destroy you. It's when you've developed that resolve that the spiritual path reveals itself to you and begins to lead you in the right direction. You'll say, "No, I will do no harm to others. I will not be a person who is aggressive and violent. But neither will I sit here and watch someone be destroyed when I know I should reach out and offer a helping hand." That's exactly what happened with me.

When the bullies saw me sitting under a tree or reading a book, for some reason they couldn't stand that, and they'd come over and kick the book out of my hand and fight me. I used to get beat up all the time. So one day I initiated this prayer in which I said, "Teach me how to defend myself." I'd read in the Bible that David was a great warrior and there was a scripture, Psalm 144, that said: "Blessed be the Lord, my strength, who teaches my fingers to fight and my hands to make war." So I said, "I'm your son; teach me, too, and I will never abuse it." Then I went out in the backyard and I began to work out and practice, believing that I would be led into the right moves and that I would come to understand. And the result of that was that eventually the bullies couldn't defeat me anymore.

Now when you take that spiritual path, the action does not come from you. I remember the first time I became aware that my body could move but that I wasn't moving it because when a person threw a punch, my hand blocked it and threw them, and I didn't even know that move. And then as I began to let go more and more, I found out that the mastery was already there; I just had to get out of the way to let it emerge, to show itself. Pretty soon I was able to use this as a platform to teach others about spirituality as a practical reality. The Japanese call it "mushin"—the art of no-mind. That's when there is no conscious attempt to act, and yet you move anyway, when the action comes from such a deep place that there is no one to take credit for it. The experience of this coexistence—of this protection that is there within you—is very powerful, and it reaffirms many of the ancient works and scriptures that say, "He who is within you is greater than he who is in the world."

WIE: How exactly is it, though, that this spiritual approach to the martial arts becomes a path to transcendence or enlightenment?

VT: Well, when you find out that you are faced with danger—when you're thinking, "What am I gonna do?"—see what happens if you say, "I'm not worried about it. I don't have to do anything. It'll be done." See what happens if you clear your mind and allow yourself to do exactly what is necessary, exactly what is correct. If you can do that, then when it's all over with, you'll discover that you're just there; you're an observer. And you'll discover that you've observed more than you've actually participated—that you have learned to still your mind so that the spirit can act. The spirit does not deliberate, only the mind does, and this is what you'll discover.

WIE: Traditionally I know it's said that from the enlightened perspective, the minute you think you are the doer—the minute you identify yourself as the one performing an action—in that moment you become the very expression of ignorance itself.

Yet even after everything you've explained, I find it difficult not to suppose that the mastery of a challenging discipline like a martial art requires a strong sense of oneself as a powerful individual, a clear and focused understanding of what one is doing, and the will and self-confidence to prevail. Looked at in this way, of course, there seems to be an inherent contradiction between enlightenment and the mastery of a martial art. But your experience seems to suggest that this simply isn't true.

VT: It isn't. It just depends on how the person approaches it. Most people approach it on a finite level—as a physical or mental ability. They develop their speed, their agility and their grace through physical exertion, working out, all those things. These are the people who come on like, "I'm the toughest guy in here. I can take all of you guys on." But the person who approaches it from the spiritual is humble, and if they were to come to him and talk that way, he'd say, "You probably could; I can see that. Look at all those muscles. Look at all that. Hey, you're too great for me." But if they were to try to attack him, they wouldn't find anybody there to attack—even though they're physically looking at the person!

I've been tested by seventh-degree black belts and other top masters, and I've asked them to explain what they feel when they attack me. They say, "It's like you're not there." They say, "I thought I had you, but then you were gone!" This is because the movement comes from a higher place and it knows what the other person is going to do. I don't know what the other person is going to do—but when they try it, they discover that it's counteracted. A lot of people say, "I want to learn your technique; it's a wonderful technique." But I say, "I don't have any techniques. Yes, you saw what appeared to be a technique.

But it's not a technique because I did not apply it. What you need to learn is how to come from that place where all the techniques already exist, and where the proper one will be there when you need it."

And I also try to teach people that there's a difference between being a martial artist and being a warrior. A martial artist is exactly what it says—a person who studies the arts of war. But a warrior is the person himself. He doesn't have to have a black belt to be a great warrior; he has the attitude of a warrior, the spirit of a warrior. And he doesn't have to be a great athlete either because he has the heart of a warrior, and the soul of a warrior, so that when the time comes, when he faces danger, he turns to steel and does what he has to do without fear.

If you're a martial artist twenty-four hours a day, seven days a week, then that's all you project and that's all you are. But if you're a warrior—if you're a father when your child comes up, a husband when your wife comes up, a friend when your buddy comes up—then you adapt yourself to all of those different roles and yet none of those roles are you. That's the kind of mind that when the battle starts, you're ready. Because you're not holding on to anything, you have everything at your disposal. That's how it works.

WIE: In your book *Soul Sword*, you describe yourself as having been "a legendary defender of the weak" who "did not hesitate to come to the rescue of victims of gangs or other practitioners of violence."

VT: Yes, I kept that promise I'd made when I prayed to God as a child. When I went up to New York in the sixties, it was completely gang-ridden, and whenever anybody was being beaten up, I never hesitated to get in the midst of the fight and take the person off of them. You see, the thing about the spirit is that the spirit can say things you would never say yourself because you know you couldn't back them up—probably you'd never even think them. So when the local gang made a circle around me in the basement of Livingstone Baptist Church after I'd been in New York for just a couple of weeks, I said, "How would you like me to handle this? Would you like it one-on-one, or do you want the group plan?" Now everybody's standing around thinking, "Boy, he's either got to be very good, or he is crazy."

Then this guy called Karate came in, their warlord, of whom people said, "He's a killer; he's been in jail for murder." I'd heard of Karate—his name was written on all the buildings in graffiti—so this was one of those movie moments. They were all saying, "He's the one, Karate! Kill him! Make an example of him!" So Karate looks at me and says, "I'm going to kill you." And I said, "Well, you may do that, but before you do, I'm going to take so many pieces out of you that forever people are going to know you were in a fight with Vernon." I looked at him and he looked at me, and then he just came up and put his arms around me. He made room at the table and said, "Get us some drinks!" He made peace with me. He offered to give me a girl—I said, "No, thank you." He offered to give me an apartment—you know, the gangs control these things. "No," I said, "I have my own, but I really appreciate the honor." So they made me an honorary warlord and they never bothered me again.

Instead of them shooting me, instead of them making an example of me, they honored me because in none of the fights that I'd been in with any of those people did I ever gloat or anything. I always helped them up and apologized, and told them that I had no desire to hurt them but that they'd put me in a position that gave me no choice. I always treated them as gentlemen, so they didn't want to kill me. It was a winning experience, you see? Because they respected me, and if anybody was to say, "Well what about this guy who came in from out of town and beat all of you up?" they'd say, "He's our warlord, he's one of us." But I wasn't no gang member; it was a compromise.

WIE: What was the source of your confidence? Has it always been the same, or did it change at some point?

VT: There's a difference between the source of my confidence, period, and my confidence in my ability to defend. They began at different times. I was born into a Christian family and we went to church all the time—I mean, when the door opened we were in! And we also had worship services in our house;

before we went to bed we had to have prayer and Bible study and all that—so I came from that kind of a family. Now what I didn't come from was a family who sat in the dark or under trees meditating, and no one could figure that out. But in that meditation, in that stillness, I connected with the source of life within me, and my relationship to that was direct, so in that quietness and stillness I felt secure and whole, and when people began to attack me, I had two feelings: One was that I knew exactly what to do to stop the attack, and the second feeling was—not wanting to hurt anybody.

Anyway, every time someone was going to hit me, I would know what was going to come, and I would also know, "I could stop this." But even with all that, I still didn't have the confidence to act. It was only when I began to seek, and to realize, that I actually got tired of getting beaten up, or tired of trying to stop a fight and getting beaten up, because by then I had discovered the means to ask God, "If you teach me, I will protect people." I'd heard about the Kitty Genovese stabbing, in Queens, and that moved me. I was only nine years old then, and I felt hurt that nobody who saw it had tried to help her. That was what triggered me to seek to be strong enough to come to the aid of anyone who was in trouble; I didn't want to pass by a person in trouble, and I would rather die in the struggle of trying to save them than walk away and die all my life knowing I'd never even tried.

So as I began to probe into this and to

practice, things began to change inside of me, and this was all part of a grand experiment in which I wasn't the one experimenting, I was simply putting together what had been there all along. See, these things were taught—they were in the Bible—and when I went to church I heard them all the time. What I began to understand was that people didn't apply the teachings to themselves. They believed that David could bring down Goliath but they didn't believe that they could. But my feeling was that the same spirit that was with David was also with me, and therefore to doubt that the spirit worked for me was to insult the Creator. In my thinking, it was very simple: If the Creator is in me also, then why am I looking at David?

WIE: You've written that a transformation in your martial arts practice occurred sometime after you met the Zen master Nomura Roshi, a transformation catalyzed by your initiation into the Zen meditation practice known as shikantaza and, in particular, by a powerful satori [awakening] you had while doing that practice. Did the goal of your martial arts practice change in any substantial way after this experience, or was it more or less the same as it had always been?

VT: The goal of my practice didn't change because I had never wanted to be a bully in the first place, and I had the ability to fight before I had that experience in shikantaza. What happened, though, is that it deepened. My early meditation had given me my own abode, but I still needed something else, and when I met Nomura Roshi, I suddenly became aware of something outside of me, something that was beyond what I was experiencing, and I saw that I needed to take a leap. I had built up walls around myself that needed to be broken down, so for two years I practiced letting go, or dropping—dropping body and mind. I remember that when I was sitting, I began to become afraid at different times because I sensed I was dying. I was very afraid. I said, "Oh, my God, I'm going to die, something is happening to me, I'm going to die." But I was advised to go ahead and die, so I decided to do just that. I said, "Well, the next time this occurs, with the life I'm living now, I'm just going to let go. I don't know what I'm doing here; what's it all about anyway? If I die, then okay."

So an initiation came through Nomura Roshi that brought me into a new level. Before, I'd been more conscious of the things that were happening. Now all of a sudden it became one with me, and there was no "art" to be known as a separate experience. I became the art, wherever I went and whatever I did.

WIE: After your realization, did you continue to practice forms?

VT: Yes, but when enlightenment hits, forms disappear; it becomes formless. Even though what you're doing is a form, you don't cling to it, and that's the difference. There are constant and endless variations on the same theme as you come to master the principle— that's the way of the spirit. You may have a principle there because the body can only move but so many different ways; but once you've mastered that principle, it's just water flowing through, and you're not interpreting it, you're following it.

WIE: Before you had this experience in shikantaza, did you already think of yourself as an individual who had "mastered himself"?

VT: I never thought of myself in those terms. In fact, it was only when I met the Roshi that, being in his presence, I saw myself. And I mean that literally. For the first time I experienced myself because his being was like my being, and therefore it was like two-way communication without a word being spoken. And in that way I became defined, in a sense, because when I was a loner, there was no one like me, and I had no way of knowing who I was. But when I saw Nomura Roshi sitting there in the park, I could feel our relationship, and all my questions being answered with no questions being asked. Then I understood that I was functioning on a plane that was different from the everyday plane that my friends and associates were functioning on—and that was my salvation because now my purpose was becoming clear. Before that, there was nobody to even give me the hint of who I was or what I was doing. All those years that I had been meditating, I had been sitting in shikantaza, without ever knowing that such a word even existed.

WIE: One could say, then, that in that meeting, you actually acquired a notion of self.

VT: Yes, but in a very different sense. "Self" with a capital "S."

WIE: In light of the discovery you've been describing, I'd like to try to distinguish in a very specific way between the two attainments we've been speaking about. It would seem that an individual who has achieved an unusual degree of self-mastery—perhaps we could again use the example of Anthony Robbins—tends to demonstrate certain qualities: charisma, confidence, positivity, creativity and a kind of dynamic freedom. He doesn't seem to be limited in the way that many people are. But all of these qualities seem to arise from the discovery—to use Robbins's words—of one's "personal power": the individual has developed a very deep conviction that could be articulated as "I Can." Enlightened individuals often seem to express similar qualities, but their source, you seem to be saying, lies in a different place—in the discovery of being itself, in "I Am."

VT: Or "Not I."

WIE: Yes, that's true. "Not I."

VT: Well, then, too, you're talking about a difference in purpose. Those who function in the capacity of a spiritual teacher, of course, would be coming from "Not I" because they are speaking from the fundamental source. But where Anthony Robbins is speaking from is the point of reception—"I've got this. I'm using it." And that's what he demonstrates. If there were music but nobody who believed they could actually play it, we wouldn't have any music, because even though music could theoretically exist, there'd be nobody with enough confidence to pick up an instrument. So on this end when a person wants to do something or achieve something and they don't have any confidence, they run to Anthony Robbins and he tells them, "You can achieve anything. If you believe in it, you can do it. Who's your example? Who would you like to be like?" He's showing them how to focus in order to get past their doubt and express something.

Now that's different from dealing with humanity in its wholeness, from trying to heal the soul of humanity. Because if you're honestly concerned with humanity in its fundamental nature, then it's not you as an individual who has the authority to speak on that; you have to become the vessel through which that is transmitted. And that's why there is this concept of "Not I," or neti neti ("not this, not this"), or "I'm just an instrument." Because it really is that way: You don't know these things, but the wisdom comes through you. Similarly, when Sant Keshavadas held me in his arms, my bond wasn't with him but through him. It was like God the Father holding me in His arms, using the body of Sant Keshavadas in order for me to be embraced by the same spirit I'd been listening to ever since I was a baby.

And now I do the same thing. When I open my arms for someone, I don't open my arms so that they can be grabbed by Kitabu; I open my arms so that God can hold them with my body—so that they can feel Him, not me. In this way, Sant Keshavadas became the link that I needed for the rest of the journey, the link that connects you to the Higher—so that no matter what's going on down here, no matter how hard the struggle gets on the bodily level, it doesn't matter. You're linked, and you have a job to do, and you understand that whatever it is that needs to be done can only be done by a human being who is willing to be God's instrument in this world. You're what the Buddha called "middle ground," precisely that point between earth and heaven where you are both and neither. And that's how you can help people: you can identify with their pain and suffering because you have pain and suffering, and yet . . . you really don't at all.

There's a sense of having always been, of experiencing this so-called "now" from a point in eternity, and experiencing the fact that if we human beings are made in the likeness of the Creator—and we are—then we are really reflections of that eternity. We may allow ourselves to become cluttered with the impermanent, but when we clean off the mirror and let it turn toward the eternal, then we realize that although we walk around in these physical shells, we're not bound to them.

WIE: In your view, is it possible for these two fundamentally different orientations toward life, "I Can" and "I Am," to coexist within a single individual?

VT: Well, they do all the time. For example, some of the greatest spiritual masters write books, and when they sit down to write those books, they have confidence in their ability to translate their experience into a publishable work that people can read and understand and enjoy. So it's coming through them—as a conduit—but at the same time, if it doesn't become personal, it has no reality base; it's just talk. So when they can say, "I had this experience, I know," then we see that it's actually possible for something that is universal to be experienced by an individual being. And as we listen to these people talk about their transformation, it begins to take place in us. It becomes real. It's no longer something beyond the cosmos that's happening totally unrelated to anybody in particular.

WIE: I understand. But I was speaking more in terms of the individual's fundamental relationship to life. Is my relationship to life based on "my ability to do something"—in other words, "I Can"—or is it based on the recognition that, "prior to anything I do or say, I exist, and that what's being expressed through me is the fact that I exist—I Am"?

It's clear from what you've just said that these two relationships to life do, practically speaking, coexist, but much of what you've said also seems to suggest that on a very fundamental level, one may at some point find oneself having to choose between them. This is not to say that action would then be excluded from one's repertoire, but that where one stands—where one locates the essence of one's being—is something that needs to be decided because what one's life is actually going to express depends upon it. Does this kind of decision accord with your own experience?

VT: Yes, in the sense that if you get even a hint of what enlightenment is, you'll give up everything for it. Because everything that isn't enlightenment is vanishing all the time. At this very moment there's hardly ground beneath our feet, and what ground there is, is vanishing as we speak. People think they're awake when they're walking around in the street, but actually they're asleep then, too. Awakening is when you see through it all—the dream when you're asleep and the one when you're "awake." Then you understand that the viewpoint we have of ourselves is based on a misconception—that because we perceive our personal experience as the ultimate reality when in fact it's not, we don't approach life as we should. That's why we need enlightenment to straighten us out. Now of course I'm not saying that you and I don't exist, or that your experience has no reality. It's not the molecules and the atoms that are going to go away, but the delusion in your mind. The molecules and the atoms will remain as hard or as soft, as light or as dark as they always were. But how you see them will be different.

WIE: Let's speak for a moment about surrender, which is traditionally thought to mean the giving up of control, whereas mastery is generally associated with the cultivation of perfect control—even more so, generally speaking, in the martial arts, where winning clearly involves asserting one's own will over the will of one's opponent. What is the role of surrender in a practice that seems to be oriented almost inevitably toward the visible demonstration of mastery and control?

VT: In a state of surrender, you're not attacking, but neither are you defending, because the action does not take place from your consciousness. On our own scale, we may look upon someone who does the Lord's bidding as a murderous person, but on the higher level where it's all played out, we are sometimes instruments, and if you are the Lord's instrument, you are not striking, which means not that you're merely saying you're not striking—you really aren't. You are not moving, but your body moves anyway, and things definitely happen. So when people say, "That was great, that was a wonderful move," you say, "Well, I cannot take credit for that. It wasn't me."

WIE: Could someone be an instrument of evil and be said to be surrendered?

VT: Yes, in the sense that if a person is an instrument of evil, then they've surrendered to evil. And if we're talking about the mastery of a particular art, or a skill that comes totally under the control of that person's ego, I suppose that's possible. But if we're talking about spiritual mastery, that's a misnomer in a way because spiritual mastery makes you an instrument of the Divine, and you could not use it to do what God would not do.

Your mastery takes the form of a servant—you reach out to people, you love people, you try to help transform them; you work with them, not against them—and you would never do anything to harm anybody because you can't make a distinction between them and you, not even if they're bad. It's all you because it's all one. If you were to attempt to harm someone, it would pain you as much as it would them because you would feel their pain, and you wouldn't want them to suffer. So it would have to be taken out of your hands, because you'd let yourself get annihilated rather than bring harm to another.

WIE: Is that what is known as the "warrior ethic"?

VT: Yes. In Bushido, the word "bu" means to cease struggling—it means that there is no one to struggle against. Now, not all warriors embrace this ideal at the highest level, but at the highest level it's said that the true master of the sword carries no sword. It isn't needed, because he's the weapon. His weapon is his continence, his stillness. His enlightenment is really something that is not of this plane at all, and for that reason it's not something that people can easily recognize. People can recognize mastery, because mastery manifests on the physical plane, but people generally don't beat a path to an enlightened person's doorstep unless they are spiritually seeking.

There are enlightened people in the world today, but most of them don't have a highway coming to their house because most people are looking for things in this world, and when they see somebody who seems to know how to get these things, they're very interested. But an enlightened person is really not that interested in this world, and in a sense the enlightened person draws people away from the world, not into it. You see, as long as you want to be in the world, and of the world, you can't really be enlightened because the demands are different. In mastery, you have to focus body and mind, and in enlightenment, you've got to let go of them.

Now the "letting go" we're talking about here is a letting go of all those preconceived concepts and limitations that frame our mind into a channel that repeats itself over and over again and keeps us from experiencing ourselves holistically. When people hear the word "surrender," they sometimes say, "Oh, if I do that, I'll have no mind!" Well, if you have no mind, you have the right mind. And it's not so much that there is no mind as that there is no preconceived concept, no defining mind, nothing there to know what mind is. It still works, though. It's still functioning. It's just that the mind that's functioning is no longer obtruding on its own self.

Then if you do something extraordinary, someone may ask, "How'd you do that?" and you'll say, "How'd I do what? What'd I do?" They'll want you to explain, but you'll know that that's a different kind of monster you'd be creating; you'd be using your mind to create "yourself" when in fact you are yourself without having to do anything at all. It's like the mirror reflecting the mirror: you see an infinite number of images, but there's really only one—and it's not in any mirror!

That's what we've been doing with our mind. We don't really know the true state of our being because we've been reflecting upon reflections that are reflections of other reflections. When we can remove all those, there'll be nothing but what is real.

WIE: When did you begin accepting challenges?

VT: When my first book of poetry, *Kung Fu: The Master*, came out in 1975, the martial arts were beginning to become quite popular, but they were always being emphasized as a violent sport. And whenever I would do talk shows, people would ask me, because of the title, "Do you do martial arts?" I'd say, "Yes, I do," and then the host would say, "Could we get a demonstration?" "A demonstration? A poet demonstrating martial arts?"—that was their idea!

So I began to do more and more of these demonstrations, but for only one reason: to point out the unlimited freedom and power of the spiritual way, of the Zen way. Then some people started talking in the martial arts world: "Is this a joke, is he a charlatan, is this for real?" So I said, "It's not me that they're attacking, it's the truth, so I'll tell you what: I'll accept any challengers, day or night, twenty-four hours a day." And then I started getting them! I accepted those challenges. I allowed people who were at the master level to challenge me, to bring me into their schools to test me; I accepted challenges on television, I even went to prisons.

A local newspaper, the *Virginian Pilot*, sponsored an event at the public arena—a night of poetry and "defense of the title"—in which I took on every challenger from every martial arts school that chose to attend, and all of them were defeated. I even allowed myself to be blindfolded! But only to demonstrate one thing—what I'd been telling them all along— It isn't me! I'm not that good! But when Zen taps the spirit within, then all things become possible. So what I was trying to show them was the potential that lies within us, not trying to say that I'm that great.

Still, you walk down the street and people say, "See him? He's the deadliest guy in Hampton Roads." I say, "No, don't say that. Please don't say I'm dangerous. I'm not dangerous." There are a lot of martial artists who are more terrifying—fancy techniques and all that kind of stuff. That's not what I represent. I go to a school; I see somebody with all the

fancy techniques and everything. I praise
them. And I say, "Strike me, hit me, kick me."
Then I knock'em down with one finger. They
say, "Well, how'd you do that?" I say, "Now
you're asking the right question! Tell me, what
did you feel when I struck you?" They say,
"Nothing." I say, "Well, if you felt nothing,
then why did you fall?" "I don't know." "Why
didn't you resist?" "I couldn't resist." I say,
"Well then, that should answer your question.
It wasn't coming from my physical body, otherwise you would have felt a blow."

That's what I try to point out to them:
"No, it's not from my physical body. Were you
just pretending? Were you just trying to make
me look good? Did you just fall on purpose?"
"No!" I've thrown policemen around in
demonstrations, three-hundred-pound policemen, with one finger. This is something that is
real.

I've often wondered how a person who was
a ninety-pound weakling could have become so
associated with the martial identity. I've tried to
draw it aside and could never do it because no
one lets me. And I think this relates back to the
karma of my own people. Sant Keshavadas
told me, "Your mission is in America, and
especially to black Americans who could bene-
fit from learning about the dharma." You see,
centuries of enslavement are also centuries of
distortion of the mind, and a misperception of
self even more profound than that which occurs
in other people because of these extraordinary
circumstances.

The most terrible thing that happened to the African American male was the loss of his sense of manhood. Every man wants to feel like he's strong enough to take care of his family, to defend his honor, to protect his loved ones. If called to go to war, every man wants to be a warrior. Nobody wants to be a wimp. But when it has been bred into you through psychological and legalistic means that you cannot raise your hand, you cannot defend yourself, that you have no right to any kind of power, then although that natural sense of manhood is still there, it becomes suppressed, and it can become self-hatred; you hate yourself for never acting on it, and you're scared because you feel surrounded by a power that you believe to be only in other people.

Well, one of my ancestors was Nat Turner, and Nat Turner was a mystic as well as a warrior. His prayers and meditations prepared him for his battle. I had a visitation from him. I saw him standing in flames with chains on, and I said, "What's wrong with you?" He said, "My people have forgotten me." And I said, "I will not forget you."

So before I can be a guru, I must first be a man. Let me express this manhood before other men, so they can see that inner light and respect me for that—then they can take in the rest. But to have a priest who is himself a wimp is not real; it doesn't go deep enough. "Turn the other cheek" means nothing at all if the other guy can slap you around at will. It only means something when you're so strong that you're gonna have to turn it for them to get to it—you just allow them, you see what I'm saying?

So what I've come to understand is that this warrior aspect is not something that I personally want; it is something that is necessary in the healing of the African American soul; it's a part of genuine manhood. And you cannot separate manhood from the spiritual part, you see, because we've always had adversaries. There are angels in the scriptures who choose to make war because if they just stood there, the other guys would own the place. They have to say, "No, you're not coming any farther than here because we're gonna stop you."

So you have the bad angel and you have the guardian angel, and the guardian angel has to be stronger than the other guy; otherwise he can't guard you. What good is a guardian angel if, when the bad ones show up, they punch him out and get you anyway? You want to be able to hide behind the guardian angel! So that's what we're talking about—being an angel—and implied in that angelic nature is the strength to defend the children of the Divine.

INDEX

ABOUT THE AUTHOR

As a young man, Vernon Kitabu Turner discovered poetry for self-expression and martial arts for self-defense. His initiation by Zen master Nomura-Roshi in 1967 changed his writing, and made him a true *Bushido* warrior.

Throughout his life, he has continued to develop his writing as both a journalist and a poet. He is recognized as a spiritual teacher by Master Sant Kesavadas of the Vishwah Dharma Mandira, and has been called "one of the most prominent voices of our time" in the international anthology, *The Way Ahead*, which featured his work along with that of the Dalai Lama and Nobel Laureate Vaclav Havel.

Hampton Roads Publishing Company

. . . for the evolving human spirit

Hampton Roads Publishing Company
publishes books on a variety of subjects including
metaphysics, health, complementary medicine,
visionary fiction, and other related topics.

For a copy of our latest catalog,
call toll-free, 800-766-8009,
or send your name and address to:

Hampton Roads Publishing Company, Inc.
1125 Stoney Ridge Road
Charlottesville, VA 22902
e-mail: hrpc@hrpub.com
www.hrpub.com